He

Walter Riggans

Christian Focus

Walter Riggans is General Director of 'The Church's Ministry Among Jewish People' and lives in St. Albans, England. He has written several books including *God's Covenant with the Jews*, *Jesus Ben Joseph*, and *Yeshua Ben David*, as well as a commentary on Numbers.

© Walter Riggans
ISBN 1 85792 328 6
Published in 1998 by
Christian Focus Publications
Geanies House, Fearn, Ross-shire,
IV20 1 TW, Great Britain
Cover design by Donna Macleod

Contents

INTRODUCTION

Most Christian teachers are agreed that along with Paul and John, the author of the work known as *Hebrews* is one of the three truly great theologians whose writings are found in the New Testament. And yet for many Christians it is a real struggle to come to terms with this work. There are complex arguments which seem to take place on some purely theoretical level; there are many quotations and references from the Scriptures, but these are not always used in ways which modern western readers appreciate; there are constant interruptions in these arguments for warnings or moral encouragements; and indeed *Hebrews* can seem quite preoccupied with ritualistic details which are no longer relevant.

Hebrews is written with a strong sense of purpose

To sit down and read *Hebrews* from start to finish is to be aware of a growing sense of momentum in the letter. While it is true that there is layer upon layer of image and meaning, the overarching purpose is never lost sight of. This is no philosophical piece, written at leisure or in an historical vacuum: rather it is an urgent response to some incident or development which has deeply disturbed the writer. We shall explore the nature of this distressing development as we work through the commentary. There are exhortations and warnings on every page, and the readers are constantly being encouraged to make decisions about the Lord and about life as his community on earth which will bring them back to the centre of God's will. This actually forms the climax of the whole letter:

May the God of peace, who through the blood of the eternal covenant brought back from the dead our Lord Jesus, that great Shepherd of the sheep, equip you with everything good for doing his will, and may he work in us what is pleasing to him, through Jesus Christ, to whom be glory for ever and ever. Amen (13:20-21).

All the details, then, fit into the overall picture without in any way detracting from the fundamental point. It is only because we are so far removed from the culture of the people addressed in *Hebrews* that we need so much help with these details. The aim of this commentary is to make that culture accessible to modern readers.

Hebrews is a sermon cum letter

Many scholars are of the opinion that *Hebrews* was originally written as a letter to a group of believers who were in need of counsel from a trusted friend. It certainly has a literary quality about it, written as it is in a quite beautiful and skilful Greek. There is no doubt that we find here the most fluent and eloquent Greek of the entire New Testament. Some scholars and preachers have even referred to it as 'the Isaiah of the New Testament' for the grandeur of its insights and language.

Of course most believers simply assume that it was composed as a letter, since there are others in the New Testament. There is no introduction, however, to show that it was a letter. We see typical introductions in Romans 1:1-7; Philippians 1:1-2; James 1:1, etc. On the other hand, the lack of an appropriate introduction is not proof that it was not a letter. The opening section could have been lost. And we must remember that 1 John is also missing an introduction, though it is certainly accepted as a letter. It should be pointed out that although most translations at 13:22 have a reference to *Hebrews* as 'a letter', the actual text does not have any such reference. The Greek simply says that the writer has written 'a few (words)', and these could have been the words of a public address.

Other scholars, therefore, do not believe that *Hebrews* was composed as a letter, but that it was first heard as an address to a group of believers. There are several references to 'speaking' in the text, as for instance the following:

> It is not to angels that he has subjected the world to come, about which we are speaking ... (2:5).

> Even though we speak like this, dear friends, we are confident of better things in your case – things that accompany salvation (6:9).

> And what more shall I say? ... (11:32).

Of course very few westerners today could keep their attention fixed on a sermon or speech of the length and complexity of *Hebrews*, but let us not forget that in that day and culture, people would have been able and willing to listen to such oratory. It is my view that what we have in our New Testament is likely to be a substantial 'sermon' delivered to a group of believers, and subsequently sent to another congregation for whom the message was equally relevant and necessary.

Hebrews is a letter whose origins are difficult to tie down

The general consensus is that the community addressed by *Hebrews* was of the line of the Hellenistic Jewish group to which we are introduced in Acts 6-7. Some even believe that this community might have been the result of the preaching and witness of those who fled during the persecutions after the death of Stephen. The key issues mentioned in Acts 6:13 at the 'trial' of Stephen, namely the role of the Temple and the Torah, certainly provide much of the substance of the debates in *Hebrews*.

But who wrote this great letter? Not a single ancient

manuscript of the letter mentions Paul as the author, and those modern translations which have Paul's name in the title are simply reflecting one of the church traditions. There is no *a priori* reason for believing Paul to be the author, though of course he might be. It may be held that *Hebrews* 2:3 militates against any apostle being responsible for writing this work, though it would have to be one of the next generation of leaders in the church.

The issue as to whether or not Paul wrote the letter rests on analysis of the radically different style of language, method of expression and doctrinal emphasis between *Hebrews* and the Pauline epistles. It does not read at all like Paul, and the fact that the manuscripts never claim that it was a Pauline epistle leads most scholars to conclude that it is simply not a Pauline epistle.

The major commentaries will lay out the analysis in full as well as giving a complete listing of the various candidates for authorship. The author was certainly someone who was thoroughly Jewish and yet who was fluent in Hellenistic thought and idiom. He was extremely sophisticated, and also very mature spiritually speaking. From about 180 AD we find claims for Pauline authorship in the *eastern* church tradition, coming in the main from church leaders and scholars in Alexandria. The north African Christian tradition, following Tertullian, tended to champion the Levite and encourager, Barnabas, as the likely author.

The *western* church tradition was very reluctant to accept Pauline authorship, and it was not until the fourth century that we find scholars and church leaders speaking about Paul as the author. Augustine tells us that he accepted Pauline authorship only on the basis of the eastern traditions for the sake of church unity. It was not a question of whether the letter was worthy of inclusion in the canon, but of whether it was written by Paul. At the Reformation, western church leaders, including Luther and Calvin, again began to question Pauline authorship. Luther's suggestion of Apollos (Acts 18:24-28) has since found many in keen agreement.

What about the dating of the letter? In particular, is there any way of knowing if the letter was written before or after the destruction of the temple in Jerusalem in 70 AD? We can begin by asserting that it was written and already enjoying a significant role within the early community of followers of Jesus by 96 AD. At that date Clement of Rome wrote an important letter to Corinth in which he referred to *Hebrews* several times. So it is certainly a first century AD letter.

Some scholars have taken verses like 10:11, written in a graphic present tense, to mean that the temple must still have been functioning. However it is clear that this could have been simply a dynamic way of highlighting the contrast between the temple service and the service given by Jesus. On the other hand, 8:13 reads like a reference to an impending fall of the temple. It also makes more sense for 13:14 to be a reference to the time while Jerusalem was still intact, since otherwise we would have expected an allusion to their destroyed city in contrast with the security of the city to come.

On the whole there is nothing in *Hebrews* which demands a dating after the fall of Jerusalem, but there is much circumstantial evidence for an earlier dating. Had the temple been destroyed already surely *Hebrews* would have made something of that fact? Instead we see his constant reference to the tabernacle, rather than to the temple, as a deliberate presentation of Jesus, not the temple, as the true fulfilment of the spirituality symbolised by the tabernacle in Israel's formative history. *Hebrews* 12:4 could be a reference to the coming destruction of Jerusalem in 70 AD. Indeed those who hold that *Hebrews* was written to a community in Rome see 10:32-34 as a reference to the persecution of the believers by Nero in Rome in 64 AD.

In any case, it is probable that *Hebrews* was written between 65 and 70 AD. The mention of Timothy in 13:23 is usually taken to mean Paul's associate, and this again puts the letter into the accepted time frame. Finally, we should point out that 2:3b suggests the time of the second generation of believers in Jesus.

Hebrews presents great spiritual teaching

There are several theological insights and emphases which are quite distinctive to *Hebrews*, and we are aware that if it were not for this book in the New Testament then we would be very much the poorer for it.

a) *Jesus is our great High Priest*. This teaching about the priesthood of Jesus after the order of Melchizedek is unique in the New Testament, and it adds a deeply enriching dimension to the development of Christology. John 17 is often referred to as Jesus' 'high priestly' prayer, and Revelation 1:13 seems to be implying high priestly vestments, but only in *Hebrews* is this teaching about Jesus as High Priest made explicit. The centrepiece of the whole work lies in its middle chapters, 7–10, and these deal with the centrality of the priestly work of Jesus on our behalf. Indeed the priestly service of the older covenant is not really comparable to the new ministry of Jesus:

• the other priests were able to serve for only a limited time, but Jesus has a permanent priesthood (7:24);

• the other priests had to serve in sanctuaries which were poor copies of the heavenly sanctuary, where Jesus serves (8:1-2, 5);

- the other priests were themselves limited by their own weaknesses and sinfulness, but Jesus is sinless (5:1-3; 7:26);

- the other priests had to offer animals as substitutes for sin, but Jesus, as the promised Servant of the Lord, offered himself as the all encompassing substitute (7:27);

- the other priests could only deal with the effects of sin, but Jesus can actually purify our inner being (9:9-10, 13-14; 10:22);

- the other priests had to repeatedly offer the sacrifices to deal with the cycle of sins, but Jesus' sacrifice of himself was offered once and for all (10:11-12);

- while it would be natural to think that all this perfection would make Jesus deficient in one respect, namely that it would mean that he cannot really sympathise with us, the opposite is in fact true (2:18; 4:15f.).

But there is even more to the teaching of *Hebrews* about Jesus' priestly ministry. It belongs to an entirely different order from that of the standard Aaronic line of succession. This is presented as part of the overall perspective of the New Covenant which Jesus inaugurated, and which we shall look at shortly. Because the new covenantal ministry of Jesus is of a higher level than that of anyone who preceded him, then even his role as priest is clearly superior to that of all previous priests (8:6). We shall deal with the importance of Psalm 110 in this High Priestly Christology in the body of the commentary.

b) *Jesus fulfilled the Day of Atonement*. Related to the previous section, it is still worth highlighting that *Hebrews* is the one book of the New Testament which really makes us focus on the truth which Paul expressed succinctly as 'Christ died for our sins' (1 Cor. 15:3). Every year the high priest was obliged to officiate at the ceremonies and sacrifices of the Day of Atonement (Lev. 16). It was as part of this momentous Day that he was permitted to enter the Holy of Holies as the climax of the drama of atonement. But even this was less than humanity needs, as shown in the fact that it all had to be repeated year after year (10:3-4).

What was needed was an atonement offering which would be effective once and for all – and this is exactly what Jesus provided. He came not only as the priest who made the offering on our behalf, but also as the very offering itself! He brought the ultimate sacrifice – 'the sacrifice of himself' (9:26). In his life, he was the complete servant of God, and his unblemished character was of a quality that no animal could match, since Jesus was able to sin, and yet resisted sin to the end. Animals were only unblemished as far as their physicality was concerned. And at the end, Jesus gave to God his perfect life, therefore fulfilling both the need for sacrifice and the desire of God for the offering of a pure and loving heart (10:5-10).

Because of Jesus' life offered to God in our place, we can now live our lives in the knowledge that we too can enter the Holy of Holies to enjoy God's presence as forgiven sinners (10:19-20).

It is worth pointing out in this context that a puzzling feature of *Hebrews* over the generations has been the lack of emphasis on the resurrection of Jesus. This is not because it was of little importance to the writer, but because *Hebrews* focuses on the typology of the Day of Atonement in its exposition of Jesus' work on the cross. The crucial aspects of the sacrificial drama were the two points of actually killing the animal and spilling its blood in the court of the sanctuary, and then presenting that spilled blood inside the sanctuary (Lev. 16).

According to the typology of *Hebrews*, these two points of emphasis correspond to the actual death of Jesus on the cross and to his presentation at the right hand of God at his ascension. Therefore the resurrection is assumed rather than highlighted in this book. *Hebrews* can be seen as an excellent complement to the major letters of Paul, which dwell on the importance of the resurrection.

c) *Jesus' ministry was the once and for all offering which we needed.* This wonderful expression, one word in the Greek, which stresses that Jesus came as the 'once and for all' offering for our sins runs like a *leitmotif* throughout the central section of *Hebrews*:

> he sacrificed for their sins **once for all** when he offered himself (7:27)

> he entered the Most Holy Place **once for all** by his own blood (9:12)

> but now he has appeared **once for all** at the end of the ages to do away with sin by the sacrifice of himself (9:26)

> we have been made holy through the sacrifice of the body of Jesus Christ **once for all** (10:10)

This is a major aspect of the Good News of Jesus – his death was completely sufficient for all of us for all time.

d) *Jesus' life was the fulfilment of the goal of Israel and all humanity.* One of the most significant Greek terms in the New Testament is *telos*, a word with a rich pedigree and a profound meaning. The word itself means conclusion or goal, and is found four times in *Hebrews*, in each case with the meaning of conclusion (3:14; 6:8; 6:11; 7:3). However the verb from which this word comes, a verb meaning 'to make complete', and other words associated with that root are much more common, and are significant in the theological vocabulary of *Hebrews*.

The perfect conclusion or goal in *Hebrews* involves the 'completion' of God's plan for the person or group concerned. Therefore all of history is moving, under God, to its completion, or fulfilment. There is nothing fatalistic or humanistic about this process, though: it is because of Jesus' life and work that we are able to move on in the power of the Spirit of God. Indeed Jesus himself underwent a process of completion, or perfection, while he lived on earth, and thus paved the way for others to follow him:

> In bringing many sons to glory, it was fitting that God, for whom and through whom everything exists, should *make* the author of their salvation *perfect* through suffering (2:10).

Note here the inseparable link between salvation and suffering in Jesus' life. It is to be no different for his followers, as we shall see. This also comes over forcefully at the end of the letter, where Jesus is called

> the *perfecter* of our faith, who for the joy set before him endured the cross, scorning its shame, and sat down at the right hand of the throne of God (12:2).

The complete life with God cannot be obtained by means of the traditional priestly process (7:11; 10:1) or the Torah in and of itself (7:19). It is Jesus who fulfils the complete life and whose atoning life permits us to share in his completion:

> by one sacrifice he has made perfect for ever those who are being made holy (10:14).

Our mark of maturity, then, is to recognise Jesus as the only complete, or perfect, person, and to seek to follow him. It is significant to realise that in 5:14 and 6:1 the words which are usually translated as 'mature' and 'maturity' are actually from this same root for completion which gives us the word *telos*.

Related to this teaching is the theology of Jesus as the great pioneer of our faith. In chapter 11 we read about the heroic men and women of faith by whom God moved salvation history on. Jesus has endured even more than any of these, and has known the worst separation from God in making our life possible. For this reason he is triumphantly called the 'Pioneer' or 'Hero' in 2:10 and 12:2.

e) *Hebrews presents Jesus as the means to complete access to God*. At the heart of true faith is the need to be able to have access to God, the Source of life and forgiveness, and *Hebrews* appreciates this perfectly. The metaphor invariably used is that of entering into the heavenly sanctuary, analogous with the high priest entering the Holy of Holies in the earthly temple. These words are wonderful:

> Let us then approach the throne of grace with confidence, so that we may receive mercy and find grace to help us in our time of need (4:16; see also 6:19-20; 7:25; 10:22; 12:22-24).

Jesus alone can break the barrier of sin which separates us from God. Jewish people already had a special access to God *vis-à-vis* other peoples as a result of God making a covenant relationship between himself and Israel, but sin was always a barrier even in that relationship. For this reason it is important for *Hebrews* to deal fully with the important passage in Jeremiah 31:31-34 which climaxes in the promise of forgiveness (see *Heb.* 8:7-13).

f) *Hebrews presents Jesus as the fulfiller of the New Covenant of Jeremiah.* This point is forcefully made in the context of Jesus' ministry as the true High Priest of his people in chapters 8-10. Jeremiah 31:31-34 is quoted in full in 8:8-12 and then part of it is quoted again in 10:16-17. This fulfilling of the covenant therefore forms the essential context in which we are to understand the sacrifice of Jesus at the heart of his service for us. *Hebrews* is drawing his readers back to their own roots, and making it clear that he is not bringing in alien concepts to their faith.

Jesus' death inaugurated the era of the New Covenant, and the readers would have benefited from this teaching that they no longer needed to depend upon the sacrificial system of the Jerusalem temple. This was a particularly important lesson to learn in the days when the war with Rome was going to lead to the destruction of the temple along with the whole city of Jerusalem. We see here a link with Jeremiah's own time, when the Babylonians were about to capture and destroy the city and temple of his day.

Just as the external expression and symbol of their faith was about to be defiled and destroyed, they were reminded of the vision of a true bonding between God and his people which would be independent of any such symbol. Real communion with God is possible without the externals. What is more, forgiveness from God, the basic need of the human heart, is also ours in Jesus, quite apart from the temple. The Jeremiah oracle climaxes in this promise of forgiveness, and it is used to this effect in *Hebrews* 8:12 and 10:17.

The new things of God, while not despising what went before, are always better, taking his people on in their walk with him. The expression 'New Covenant' could just as well be translated from the Hebrew as 'Renewed Covenant'. It is tragic that so many Christians view the newness of Jesus' life and the life of the community of those who follow him in such a way that they jettison what went before as now worthless. Each covenant which we see in Scripture presupposes and builds upon those which preceded it, and the covenant promised to Jeremiah is no exception. In the opening chapter of *Hebrews* we are taught that the prophets and angels are not to be compared with Jesus, so inferior are they to him as a means of revelation. But we should not marginalize them nor disparage their continuing importance. In the same way, the covenants in Scripture still have a vital place (Matt. 5:17-19).

Jeremiah speaks of the covenant involving God's laws (31:33), being summed up in a covenant formula (31:33), enabling people to know God (31:34), and enabling the forgiveness of their sins (31:34). All of this represents realities which they could have been experiencing already! It was a change of heart which was needed above all, as Jeremiah knew only too well, and *Hebrews* explains that this change is what Jesus has made altogether possible.

g) *Hebrews emphasises the significance of Jesus' humanity.* Jesus was descended from the tribe of Judah (7:14); he was made like his brothers in every way (2:17); he knew the full force and venom of temptation, being able to resist it right up to its maximum power (2:18; 4:15); he knew the pain and the lessons of suffering (2:10; 5:8; 12:3); he knew the need for prayer (5:7); and he depended on the love and power of his Father to raise him from the dead (13:20).

Jesus was not simply a divine being who appeared to be human merely to represent humanity before God. He really gave up his own body and blood for our sakes (10:19-20; 13:12). It is only in appreciating his full humanity that we can begin to sense his divinity. Jesus is as close to us as could be, and is able to take us into the very presence of God, our Father.

Jesus is the unique and incomparable Son of God (1:1-4).

But if he is the Son of God's house, then we who are his are that house, and we are in relationship with him (3:6). This enables him to bring us, the sons (and daughters!) who are far below him, to share glory with him (2:10-13). As the Son acts as our Mediator before God (5:1-10), so we can act as sons in terms of our commitment to righteousness (5:11-6:8). As the Son endured (12:1-2), so we can endure as sons (12:3-29). As the Son suffered for us (13:12), so we can suffer as sons (13:13-16). We can follow where he leads because we recognise in him not only the glory of God but also the identification with us.

Hebrews insists on the foundational nature of the Old Testament

For many Christians the Old Testament functions as little more than background, sometimes interesting sometimes not, sometimes helpful sometimes not, for the New Testament. This is to completely misunderstand the nature of Scripture and the relationship between the two Testaments. The Old is the indispensable foundation of the New. For this reason increasing numbers of Christians are beginning to adopt the practice of Jewish believers in Jesus of referring to the Old Testament as the Hebrew Bible. This avoids the implication of irrelevance or relative unimportance for the Scriptures which came before the birth of Jesus. *Hebrews* certainly emphasises the need for the Hebrew Bible in the life of followers of Jesus.

Hebrews depends on the Hebrew Bible because it is the very word of God himself. This is the case for passages where God is said to be speaking (e.g. Ps. 110:4, cited in *Heb.* 5:6), and passages where some human being is actually doing the speaking in the original context (e.g. Deut. 32:43, cited in *Heb.* 1:6; Ps. 104:4, cited in *Heb.* 1:7). It is all the word of

God. Sometimes *Hebrews* takes passages and applies them directly to Jesus or to the community of believers (e.g. 1:5-14; 3:7-19; 12:5-12). At other times he applies the principles to be found in Scriptural passages (e.g. 6:13-16; 11; 12:14-17).

There are actually 37 quotations from the Hebrew Bible, and a further 70 or so clear allusions to passages in the Hebrew Bible, which gives a good indication of the importance of the Hebrew Bible to *Hebrews* and his community. In particular we see that the Book of Psalms is fundamental to the thought of *Hebrews*. Psalms 2, 104, 45, 102 and 110 are used in chapter 1; Psalm 8 is used in chapter 2; Psalm 95 is used in chapters 3 and 4; Psalm 110 is used in chapters 5 and 7; Psalm 40 is used in chapter 10. This further reinforces the perspective that he comes from a priestly family and reflects priestly concerns – the Book of Psalms was, of course, the song and prayer book of the temple.

One issue of major importance must be mentioned here, however, although it will be dealt with more fully in the commentary itself. *Hebrews* and his readers were at home in the Septuagint, the name given to the ancient Greek version of the Hebrew Bible. (This version is commonly referred to by its abbreviation, LXX.) In the third century before the birth of Jesus the Jewish communities outside of the land of Israel were more fluent in Greek than Biblical Hebrew, and so they commissioned an official version of the Bible. Jewish scholars undertook this labour of love for Jewish communities. It is of considerable importance to note that in many places there is a marked difference between the Hebrew and Greek texts.

Jewish community leaders have long accused Christians of tampering with the original text of the LXX, either deliberately for the purpose of creating texts more suitable for their own faith, or accidentally through incompetence with the Hebrew language and idiom. Christians, followed in general by western scholarship, have traditionally held that the LXX was originally a tendentious version anyway, taking liberties with the Hebrew text when it suited them. However the consensus today among scholars, both Jewish and Christian, is that the LXX may well represent a translation of a Hebrew text which was itself different from the one which has come down to us as the authoritative text of Scripture.

The version of Scripture which is more commonly used in *Hebrews* is that of the LXX, not the received Hebrew text (known as the Masoretic Text). Does this simply reflect the fact that *Hebrews* was writing to a Diaspora community which itself would be more at home with Greek, and which probably used the LXX in its study of the Bible? Or is there a case to be made, as many scholars do, for seeing *Hebrews* using the LXX when its version of a passage suited his teaching point better? We shall need to note these points in the text when we come to them. Here is one example to show what is being referred to here.

In *Hebrews* 8:8-12 we have a quote from Jeremiah 31:31-34. The Hebrew text of verse 32b is correctly translated by the NIV as follows:

> because they broke my covenant, though I was a husband to them, declares the Lord.

The LXX of these words reads as follows:

> because they did not remain faithful to my covenant, and I turned away from them, declares the Lord.

We note that *Hebrews* 8:9b follows the LXX reading here. The issue is thereby raised as to whether the Lord did turn away from his people. But at another level altogether we are faced with the matter of the implications of *Hebrews* using text other than the accepted Hebrew text of the Bible. Our Bible translators are also beginning to prefer the LXX and other ancient versions at various points in the Scripture, and we need to be alerted to the significance of this development.

Hebrews bridges two cultures – to whom was it written?

As I have said above, *Hebrews* contains the purest and best Greek in the New Testament. This is obvious not only from the vocabulary and ease of expression, but also from the fluent use of rhetorical styles and structures which were employed in Hellenistic culture. Again, we shall see this in the commentary. Greek philosophy was constantly wrestling with the notion that there was a perfect world somewhere of which our world is an imperfect copy. The perfect world is the only reality, and our world is a mere shadow, or reflection. Therefore to those immersed in Greek ways and thought *Hebrews* proclaimed that the search for reality was over – it had been found in Jesus.

But this is not the whole story – nor would it be sufficient. The Jewish community had developed its own characteristic method and style of dealing with Scriptural texts, a method known as midrash. *Hebrews* cannot be fully understood apart from an appreciation of the midrashic rhetoric used in its dealings with Scripture. It is highly likely that *Hebrews* began as a synagogue-type sermon given by a learned and experienced leader to a group of Jewish believers. Besides, *Hebrews* perfectly understands the heart of the Jewish people's wrestling in life: how can we find the way to a full relationship with the holy God? Therefore *Hebrews* proclaims that the search is over – it has been provided in Jesus.

The only geographical reference in the letter is to 'Italy' (13:24), but this does not help us particularly since it would refer to the place from which the letter was written rather than to which it was written. However the text actually says that 'those from Italy' send greetings, so they might have been living anywhere at the time. Because of this lack of real geographical help from the body of the letter, scholars have made various suggestions as to the location of the community which received this letter: Jerusalem, Rome, Antioch, Ephesus, Alexandria, Caesarea, and others. The major commentaries can be consulted for full discussion of this point.

This second generation community (2:3) was in trouble from heretical and/or misguided teaching (e.g. 1:1-2:4; 13:9-10). Neither were they immune from serious moral problems (e.g. 13:4-5). They were losing a properly respectful attitude towards their leaders (13:7-8, 17). On top of all this some of the community was even losing the motivation to gather with everyone for worship and mutual encouragement (10:25). They were sorely in need of encouragement to persevere in their faith in spite of troubles (10:36; see the context of 10:32-35).

Strictly speaking, for many, the title 'To the Hebrews' would not be a way of referring to all Jewish people at that time. It would have been restricted to Jewish people for whom Hebrew was the first language and who were relatively successful in resisting the worst extremes of Hellenistic culture (see Acts 6:1; 9:29). But this proves to be quite ironic in the present context, since most scholars see the ethos of *Hebrews* as being a Hellenistic Jewish one. And we also need to remember that Paul called himself a 'Hebrew of the Hebrews' (Phil. 3:5) even although he was from Tarsus. So it is probably right simply to assume that this letter was written to a community of Jewish believers in Jesus who were in some danger of falling back into some other form of Jewish faith and practice.

Certain scholars have tried to show that the recipients of the letter were in fact non-Jews, but there is nothing in it to really support this view. We find no attack on pagan beliefs or practices. Why would the author focus so heavily on passages from the Hebrew Bible, assuming, as he does, that such appeals will make a significant difference, if he was writing to non-Jews? This was a community of Jewish believers in Jesus who were learning to live as such in an increasingly hostile environment.

Perhaps there is therefore a play on words in the title, in that the word 'Hebrews' comes from a root which means to cross over an area, to wander. This would sit nicely with the word of encouragement to these 'biological Hebrews' who needed to learn about their true goal and home in life:

> For here we do not have an enduring city, but we are looking for the city that is to come (13:14).

In our day there is growing interest in the view that this community was specifically composed of Jewish people from an Essene background, like those who lived at Qumran and who left us the famous Dead Sea Scrolls. They had a well developed view of the importance of angels; they pioneered a whole system of special ceremonial meals; they held Melchizedek in the utmost honour; they spoke of two Messianic figures, one the royal Davidic king, but the other a priestly leader; they valued a part of the apocryphal book of Ecclesiasticus which described the history of the faithful and the faithless people of Israel; and they stressed that they were the community of the new covenant. These are all important issues in *Hebrews*, as we shall see.

Conclusion

What we have here in *Hebrews* is a remarkably rich and challenging communication from a spiritually mature and intellectually sophisticated pastor to a struggling community of Jewish believers in Jesus. He knew them, loved them, and suffered with them in their desire to make their stand for Jesus in a world which was going to become increasingly intolerant of them. We have a great deal to learn from this letter!

Select Bibliography

Barclay, William: *The Letter to the Hebrews* (The Saint Andrew Press, Edinburgh, second edition, 1957)

Brown, Raymond: *The Message of Hebrews* (IVP, Leicester, 1982)

Bruce, F.F.: *Commentary on the Epistle to the Hebrews* (Eerdmans Publishing Co., Grand Rapids, Michigan, 1964)

Lindars, Barnabas: *The Theology of the Letter to the Hebrews* (Cambridge University Press, Cambridge, 1991)

Montefiore, Hugh: *A Commentary on the Epistle to the Hebrews* (Adam & Charles Black, London, 1964)

COMMENTARY

1. Superior to the Prophets (1:1-2)

The clear teaching of these opening verses is that Jesus is incomparably better than all that went before him. *Hebrews* actually uses the term for **superior** twelve times throughout the letter, from 1:4 to 12:24. This is a key matter of revelation – Jesus is greater than anyone or anything to which he might be compared.

The Muslim call, 'Allah hu aqbar', which Christians usually assume means, 'God is Great', is actually very clever indeed. I am not trying to elevate the Muslim faith, but just to point out something of importance as we come to this letter. The Arabic phrase actually means, 'God is Greater.' If you ask a Muslim, 'Greater than what?', the answer given is, 'Greater than anything you care to name.' This claim made by Muslims for Allah is in fact true only for Jesus!

Much of Jewish thought in Jesus' day supposed that all time and life was divided into two ages – known as the present age and the age to come. The present age is one of struggle and defeat, but the age to come will see God's perfect order and joy established in the world. The 'Day of the Lord' separates the two ages, bringing about **these last days**, and it is the time when the Messiah enters history and brings the age to come into reality. Jesus has done exactly that.

According to Jewish beliefs, the last of the biblical prophets was Malachi, who died centuries before Jesus was born. The Jewish people and the world needed the Messiah to come to live out the life of God among us. **The prophets** spoke about God's love, glory and power, etc., but Jesus personified it all.

The prophets were God's great messengers before the coming of the Messiah, but now God is able to communicate with us at the deepest level because **his Son** has come and begun the supernatural transformation of the world. So we note that *Hebrews* focuses on the status of Jesus as God's own Son – his mission, reign, obedience and perfect nature (1:2,3,5,8; 3:6; 4:14; 5:8; 7:3,28). The age to come has already begun. As Jesus said after his baptism: 'The time has come. The kingdom of God is near. Repent and believe the good news!' (Mark 1:15)

All of the **various ways** added together would not begin to compare with the depth and richness of revelation which has come in Jesus.

God so loves the Son that he has made him the **heir of all things**. This goes far beyond the promise of inheriting the nations of the earth given in Psalm 2:8, a Psalm which is used in this opening chapter of *Hebrews*. Only God can give this gift to Jesus (Matt. 4:8-10), and those who fully share Jesus' life are also promised a share in this inheritance with him (Rom. 8:17).

Hebrews delights to reveal that Jesus inherits what he was instrumental in creating in the first place. The Son is the one **through whom** (God) **made the universe**. Paul and John also teach us this important truth (Col. 1:16; John 1:3). This letter has been written to believers in trouble, but just as Jesus was the means by whom God created order and beauty out of the primeval chaos, so he will be able to bring stability and purpose to the difficult life of believers then and now.

2. Superior to the Angels (1:3-14)

It is worth pausing for a moment to draw attention to the way in which *Hebrews* is saturated in the teaching of the Hebrew Bible. The opening chapter is already full of references and allusions, and we note in particular the value given to the Psalms as a treasure house for revelation about the Son of God. The Scriptures of the Jewish people are simply assumed to be centred upon and pointing towards Jesus. Jesus himself gave the lead in this interpretation on the way to Emmaus (Luke 24:27).

It was important to *Hebrews* to establish at the outset that
the angels, though a wonderful creation of God's, were far
below Jesus in authority and glory. By Jesus' time the Jewish
people had a sophisticated theology of angels who served as
the mediators between the transcendent God in heaven and
his people on earth below. There was even the belief in some
quarters that angels carried Israel's prayers to God. Perhaps
the believers to whom *Hebrews* was written came from a
background which highlighted the significance of angels, and
therefore needed to be given particular help.

There is in fact only one mediator – the Son of God himself
(see 1 Tim. 2:5-6).

The Son's **name** is superior to that of the angels, and this
refers to his status and authority. In Philippians 2:9-11 we
learn that God gave Jesus 'the name that is above every name',
the very name of 'Lord'. This was the title reserved by Jewish
people for God himself!

We must remember that the angels are part of God's
creation, and therefore cannot be compared with the eternal
Son. This contrast is alluded to in verses 7-9. The Son's throne
is everlasting, but the angels come and go like **winds** or **flames
of fire**. Two famous Jewish texts relate angels to wind and
fire in this way (4 Ezra 8:20-21; Yalkut Shim'oni 2:11:3).

The Hebrew term for angel is simply a word which means
a 'messenger', and at the end of the day that is what angels
are. They are **ministering spirits sent to serve**. But note the
grace of God in that he also sends his angels to serve those
who belong to Jesus. The early believers knew about the reality
of angels in their lives as we see in the book of Acts (5:19,
8:26, 10:3, 12:23, 27:23-24).

The angels actually live to **worship** and serve the Son. The
reference here in verse 6 is to the Greek version of the Hebrew
Bible (the Jewish Septuagint), and could be from
Deuteronomy 32:43a or Psalm 97:7b. The Hebrew text doesn't

use the term for angels, but speaks of 'gods'. We are taught here that Jesus is worthy of the same worship as God the Father.

Jesus is worthy because he is **the radiance of God's glory**. The word for radiance can mean a bright reflection, or as is more likely here, a shining forth. In Israel's history the glory of God was an almost visible manifestation of the overpowering presence of God. It guided them and assured them of God's blessing (see Exod. 24:15-17; 33:18-23; Lev. 9:5-6, 23). This glory is now seen overwhelmingly in the person of Jesus.

Jesus is also worthy because he is **the exact representation** of God's being. In 2 Corinthians 4:4 and Colossians 1:15 Jesus is described as the 'image' of God, using a word which gives us the English term, 'icon'. However *Hebrews* uses a word which occurs nowhere else in the New Testament, and which gives us the English word, 'character'. It is a word which means the exact detail and expression of the original. If we want to know what our Father is like then we pay attention to Jesus.

After ... he sat down shows us that, worthy and glorious though the Son is, there is a sense in which the Father honoured and glorified him even more when he proved his love for us by dying for our sins on the cross. It was 'after' he purified us that he sat in the place of honour **at the right hand** of the Father. This staggering truth is developed throughout *Hebrews,* as elsewhere (see Phil. 2:9).

Right at the opening of the letter the readers are encouraged to remember that this Jesus will never change, and that he will be with them in every situation (12b). This was a word of comfort which Jesus himself gave to his disciples (Matt. 28:20b), and it also helps to close *Hebrews* (13:8). We need to hold on to that same promise.

3. Therefore we dare not ignore Jesus, the Word of God (2:1-4)

We are urged to **pay more careful attention** to the word of God brought to us in Jesus because otherwise we are in danger of missing our only hope for salvation. In fact the vocabulary used in verse 1 is also used to speak about mooring ships (as well as paying attention) and the drift caused by winds and tides if ships are not moored (as well as drifting in attention). If we don't anchor ourselves in the word of God then we can miss the only safe haven there is – namely Jesus himself.

The community which received this letter was evidently in need of this warning, since there are no less than five such warnings in the letter (2:1-4; 3:7-4:13; 5:11-6:12; 10:19-39; 12:1-13:22). Here they are alerted to the twin attitudes of **violation and disobedience**. The first word refers to crossing a line which has been clearly drawn – wilful breaking of laws. The second term was originally used of flawed hearing, then what might be called half-hearted listening, and finally the attitude of purposefully filtering out what the hearer did not want to hear. It is about closing one's ears to God's voice.

The real question is, '**how shall we escape if we ignore such a great salvation**'? It is important that we realise that people do not spend eternity in separation from God because of the sin of rejecting Jesus. That fate comes to people who do not let Jesus rescue them from it. We are all sinners by definition, and are all heading for eternal punishment unless Jesus rescues us – this is the meaning of salvation.

In one sense this salvation is already a reality for those who belong to Jesus (2:10; 5:9), and in another sense the full rescue is yet to come (1:14; 6:9; 9:28).

The **signs, wonders and various miracles** were the classic testimonies to the truth of the Gospel which was preached by the apostolic witnesses. The same three words are found in

Acts 2:22 and 2 Corinthians 12:12. But we must also note
Acts 2:43; 4:30; 5:12; 6:8; 14:3; 15:12.

As Paul writes at one point, **the gifts of the Holy Spirit**
are all given by the one Holy Spirit for the sake of the
community of believers (1 Cor. 12:4,11).

The full gospel is that Jesus can transform our lives by
rescuing us from certain death, and that the Holy Spirit can
further transform our new lives with gifts which he deems
appropriate for us.

4. Jesus will be exalted over all (2:5-8a)

Angels are important to *Hebrews*, because they were clearly
very significant for the recipients of the letter. Some Jewish
groups believed that angels were instrumental in bringing
God's word to Israel, a belief expressed in the Septuagint
version of Deuteronomy 33:2, which mentions angels where
the original Hebrew does not. The focus on angels was
particularly marked by the community of pious Jews who lived
at Qumran, on the shores of the Dead Sea, and *Hebrews* may
have been written to a group of such people who became
believers in Jesus.

Those Jewish people held that the present age was largely
under the administration of angelic hosts, led by Michael, and
that in the age to come the influence of angels would be even
greater. *Hebrews* acknowledges that in this age people are **a
little lower than the angels**, quoting from Psalm 8, and indeed
includes the incarnate Jesus in this diminished role *vis-à-vis*
the angels. But then *Hebrews* insists that in **the world to come**,
when the purposes of God have been fulfilled, it will be Jesus
alone who is in authority.

5. Therefore we can trust him now for ultimate victory (2:8b-10)

The little word **yet** may not seem to be very theological, but it is a key word in this section. The truth is that Jesus' Lordship is not self-evident. **But we see Jesus** means that we trust Jesus for the future because what we do know about him is already enough to give us grounds for trust.

He goes before us and we are ready to follow him, trusting him. *Hebrews* uses a wonderful expression for Jesus in this context. It calls him **the author** of salvation, which is a translation of a Greek term perhaps better translated by 'pioneer'. It is also used of Jesus in *Hebrews* 12:2 and Acts 3:15; 5:31. It can mean the chief of a group of people, the founder of a city, the person responsible for establishing a school of thought, or someone who blazes the trail for others to follow. Jesus has returned to his place at the right hand of the Father and has opened up the way for us to follow him there.

But that way is a difficult and painful one, not one of escape from suffering. Jesus will only enjoy the highest exaltation because he willingly became lower than the angels and **suffered death** among us. His suffering is highlighted again in 2:18; 5:8 and 13:12. This is the message also of Revelation 5:9-10 and Philippians 2:6-10, where a key word is the 'therefore' of verse 9. Jesus identifies fully with us in our suffering, and this was a vital lesson for *Hebrews*' community to learn since they themselves were experiencing serious persecution for their faith.

There are several places in the New Testament where we are encouraged to reflect on the truth that suffering can lead to a significant increase in our maturity as believers (see Jas. 1:2-4; 1 Pet. 1:6-9). We learn to be more like Jesus and we become more able to empathise with and help others who find themselves in various kinds of crisis.

However, something extraordinary is said here in *Hebrews*. We are told that Jesus himself was made **perfect through suffering**. It is vital that we avoid the mistake of thinking that this 'perfection' was in the realm of morality. Jesus was always morally and spiritually sinless (see *Heb*. 4:15; 7:26; 2 Cor. 5:21; 1 Pet. 2:22; 1 John 3:5).

The word translated as **perfect** is from a root which in the New Testament means perfectly fulfilling one's purpose. It is helpful to think about the difference between the potential for fulfilment and the actual realisation of that potential. An engineer may design something which should work perfectly, but only when it has actually worked perfectly in a real life situation will he pronounce it as perfect. A botanist may grow a plant with what looks like a perfect bud, but only when it actually blossoms will she really know that it was perfect.

In the same way, *Hebrews* teaches us that Jesus somehow fulfilled the potential vast supply of love and commitment for us (which his Father never doubted) when he actually triumphed in prayer at Gethsemane (Matt. 26:39) and went to the cross on our behalf (John 19:30). How could any of us dare to think that we could go through life without sharing in Jesus' sufferings as well as his joy? In the light of what he has gone through for us, how could we ever fail to trust him in every situation?

6. Jesus calls us his family (2:11-16)

Through a Messianic interpretation of Psalm 22 and Isaiah 8 *Hebrews* teaches that all who believe in Jesus are regarded as his brothers and sisters. Jesus identified with us in his earthly life, and his life among us was so real and so intensely lived that he is even now able to fully sympathise with each of us. He is there with us not only in the times of joy and satisfaction but also in our suffering and struggles with temptation. If he himself had not known these experiences then he would not be able to really help us when we need his help.

Note that just as *Hebrews* has put the angels in their proper perspective in verse 5 of this chapter, so we find the stress here in verse 16 that Jesus did not come to help the angels, but **Abraham's descendants**. Angels are not subject to the same uncertainties of life and faith; they do not face the challenge of death; and they are not prey to those who seek to persecute the Lord's people. In other words, the full drama of salvation is played out in the human realm, and in particular in the life of Israel.

The phrase, **Abraham's descendants** is found in Isaiah 41:8-16, and this is a rich context for our understanding of the *Hebrews* passage. The whole Isaiah passage is about Israel as the chosen 'servant' of God, and Abraham's descendants there are encouraged not to be afraid of those who are set to oppose them. The Lord says that he will strengthen and 'help' them. The servant people of God need his understanding and protection. The Believers to whom *Hebrews* was written also needed this same **help** from the Lord.

All the same, it is possible at times for us to become so depressed by our fears and inadequacies that we find it hard to really accept that we belong with Jesus. At other times we can become so defeated by our inability to overcome temptations that we fear that Jesus might be reluctant to welcome us into his presence. How could he be happy in our company, as it were?

At times like this we should remember and rejoice in the truth of verse 11. **Jesus is not ashamed** of us – he calls us his brothers and sisters in spite of the fact that we are going through a long and sometimes difficult process of sanctification. The fact is that this process is very important to *Hebrews*, and recurs throughout the letter. Paul emphasises the necessity of being 'justified' by God, but *Hebrews* focuses on the role of Jesus as our 'High Priest', and so has a special interest in the issues of holiness.

Jesus came to deal with our alienation from God. Therefore he had to deal with sin and death, and therefore he had to deal with the work of **the devil**. Death is shown in the Bible to be the result of sin, and our last and greatest enemy (Gen. 2:17, 3:3-4; Rom. 5:12, 6:23; 1 Cor. 15:21, 26, 56; Rev. 20:14). Not surprisingly, death is within the realm of the devil. It represents the devil's final claim to power over our lives. Jesus had to do away with this power and its hold over us, and so he came to **destroy** the devil.

As it is put in Colossians 1:13, God has 'rescued us from the dominion of darkness and brought us into the kingdom of the Son he loves'. We are safely accepted into the family of Jesus.

7. Jesus is our High Priest (2:17-18)

We shall leave for a more appropriate moment the clear tension that there seems to be in recognising Jesus as Israel's true **high priest**. The priests were all supposed to come from the tribe of Levi, and yet Jesus came from the tribe of Judah! Much of the letter is devoted to explaining this enigma and to helping us to realise the beauty of God's plan in bringing the kingly and priestly roles together in Jesus (see 3:1-6; 4:14-5:10; 6:19-10:22).

A deeply important issue is reflected in this passage, and we should make sure that we reflect on it. Jesus came to **make atonement** for our sins. The Greek word used here can either mean to make 'expiation' or 'propitiation'. The former idea is of sins being covered over, as it were, and dealt with in this manner. They are now out of sight and out of God's mind. The latter idea is of the offended party – in this case God –

being appeased. The basic problem is seen as not so much sins having to be covered but God's holy and righteous wrath having to be turned away from us.

The translation of the NIV suggests the former understanding of this text, whereas its footnote introduces the possibility of the latter interpretation. We perhaps need to learn that both of these dimensions of what Jesus accomplished on the cross are of vital importance for us. He reconciled us to God (propitiation) and dealt with the sin in our lives (expiation). But what we must *not* be deceived into believing is that our Father was in any sense reluctant to love or forgive us.

Jesus brought about the reconciliation which was necessary because of the sin in our lives which blocked the Father's full blessing of us. However the Gospel was the Father's plan, not one which Jesus devised in order to save us from an uncaring God. John 3:16 teaches that *God* so loved us that he sent Jesus to save us. We have just read here in *Hebrews* 2:10 that *God* decided to work through Jesus in bringing us to glory.

We should be careful about the message we might be sending unawares when we use posters and car stickers which say: 'Thank God for Jesus!' Jesus is our High Priest, and this is a wonderful picture of Jesus as our great mediator. Priests were mediators between God and the people of Israel, representing each before the other. The New Testament is clear that Jesus is the Mediator who makes possible the purpose of our Father in heaven (see 1 Tim. 2:5-6). Jesus had no agenda nor goal in life which was not our Father's purpose.

This is not at all to devalue Jesus, but to present the reality of the loving relationship between Father and Son which we see in the Scriptures. We shall have cause to see this featured again in the letter to the *Hebrews*.

8. Jesus is superior to Moses (3:1-6)

In the first two chapters of this letter the focus has been on Jesus' superiority over the angels who played such a vital role in the previous theology of this community of Jewish believers. Now the emphasis shifts to Jesus' superiority over Moses, the founding prophet, as it were, of the Torah faith of the Jewish community. Numbers 12:6-7 shows us God's high esteem for Moses. This is the source of the reference to Moses being **faithful in all God's house**. We still speak of people founding a 'house' or dynasty.

Note that Moses is set apart from all other prophets in that Moses heard God in a direct way of some sort and saw 'the form of the Lord'. The Jewish community then and now would find it hard to imagine how anyone could get closer to God than this. It is important for *Hebrews* to meet the challenge that Moses might still be the high prophet for Jewish believers in Jesus. Jesus is not only the supreme King and High Priest of Israel, but he is also the supreme Prophet. Therefore although it might seem like an anticlimax to some Christians to move from angels to Moses, this was a significant point for *Hebrews* to make.

Of course Moses was only a **servant** in God's house. God's eulogy for Moses, if we can call it that, stresses this fact: 'Moses my servant is dead.' (Josh. 1:2). There is no dishonour in being a servant of God – quite the contrary – but it cannot compare with being God's Son.

The Son is faithful in welcoming us to be part of God's household (verse 6). This metaphor is used elsewhere in the New Testament, and expresses a key truth for us to learn (see Eph. 2:19-22; 1 Tim. 3:15; 1 Pet. 4:17). We are brothers and sisters of Jesus (2:11, 17; 3:1) whom he loves and acknowledges. But more than this, we are honoured by the extraordinary title of **holy brothers**. This is as a result of Jesus' work in us (2:11).

The root meaning of the Hebrew term behind the biblical concept of 'holiness' is of separateness from everyday life and use. People, objects or places which are described as holy are holy by association with the Lord – since only he is holy in and of himself. When someone or something is set apart for the service of God then it is holy. Therefore although the process of becoming holy (sanctification) is a lifelong one, with none of us ever reaching a fully sanctified state here on earth, in another sense we become holy as soon as we commit our lives to the Lord and his service.

This is why *Hebrews* can go on immediately to say that the holy brothers are those **who share in the heavenly calling**. We are now on a different (separate) path from the one on which we were walking, even though we may be only at the start of our journey on that path. The word translated by the phrase 'who share in' is one which appears elsewhere in the letter (3:14; 6:4; 12:10). It focuses on the blessing or the privilege which is shared rather than on anything which the sharers might have in common in themselves. Once again we see the reinforcement of the teaching that we have nothing in ourselves to boast about: we are holy because of the fact that we belong to the Lord.

Therefore it is appropriate that *Hebrews* says to his congregation: **fix your thoughts on Jesus**. The term means to focus one's attention firmly on the matter at hand in order to fully comprehend the lessons to be learned. Jesus himself urged this same attitude in his teaching (see Luke 12:24, 27 where the term found here in *Hebrews* is also found. It is also used in *Hebrews* 10:24 to emphasise the need to really care enough for our brothers and sisters to work hard at helping them to live lives for the Lord). In the case of *Hebrews* 3:1 we are taught that only Jesus can make the necessary difference in our lives, and so we must commit ourselves to him in order to find salvation.

Hebrews employs here a title for Jesus which is unique in the New Testament. He refers to him by the title **apostle**. The term literally means 'someone who is sent out'. In Jesus' day it was used in the Jewish community to refer to the envoys of the Sanhedrin, the high court of the Jewish religious authorities. It also came to be used in the same way that we would speak of 'ambassadors' from one nation or authority to another.

The 'apostle' was invested with the complete trust and authority of the person who sent him. He spoke for his master. To receive him was to receive his master, and in the same manner, to abuse or reject the apostle was to insult and reject the master.

The consequence of rejecting Jesus as God's great apostle is more serious than anything else could possibly be. To reject the apostle is to reject the one who sent him. As we think again of Moses we remember the passage where God promises to send another prophet like Moses (Deut. 18:15-19). This superior prophet will have God's very words put in his mouth, as we read there, and God says: 'If anyone does not listen to my words that the prophet speaks in my name, I myself will call him to account.'

Moses was also called and 'sent out' by God (Exod. 3:4, 10, 14), but his mission was but the shadow of the greater Exodus which Jesus undertook on our behalf. Our part in this wonderful journey with Jesus is to trust him and believe all his words and deeds. As *Hebrews* puts it, we are to **hold on to our courage and ... hope.** Ours is to follow where he leads.

9. We dare not harden our hearts (3:7-19)

The quoting of Psalm 95 at this point in the letter is in keeping with the focus on Moses. In the book of Exodus, during the time when Moses was pleading with the Pharaoh to let the

people of Israel go to worship the Lord, we read that God sent
a series of plagues to persuade the Pharaoh to surrender his
will to God's. However, a constant refrain is that the Pharaoh
'hardened his heart' and would not let them go (e.g. Exod.
8:19, 32).

But we cannot assume that hard hearts are only possible
for people who do not belong to the Lord. Moses also
experienced the Israelites hardening their hearts in the
wilderness after their liberation from Egypt. In the previous
section of the letter we saw the reference to Numbers 12:6-7,
where Moses is praised as a faithful servant of God. These
verses are found in the middle of the section of Numbers 11–
16 where the Israelites are repeatedly complaining about God's
treatment of them.

The climax of this ongoing hardening of their hearts to the
providential care of God came when the people vented their
frustration at having no obvious source of water. The Lord
was angry with them and the place was marked by the names
Massah and Meribah, the Hebrew terms for 'testing' (the
Lord) and 'quarreling' (see Num. 20:1-13; Exod. 17:1-7). This
terrible event was so significant that it is referred to in Psalm
95, to be remembered every time the Psalm is used in private
or public worship.

Hebrews uses the appropriate part of the Psalm to warn his
readers not to become guilty of the same hardening attitude.
This was a community of believers who were living in very
difficult days, and it might have been hard not to wonder if
God would really provide for them at every turn. God was so
angry with that first generation after the Exodus that he vowed
that they would not enter his rest (verse 11). Here we have the
first generation after the greater Exodus which Jesus brought
about and they must be careful not to repeat the same sinful
mistake (verse 12).

The word translated as **turns away from** in verse 12 is a

very strong one, implying desertion and betrayal. It gives us the English word 'apostasy', and some of these Jewish believers might have been in danger of just that. This word therefore speaks about an attitude which is worse than simply being negligent or ignorant. The momentum of words used in *Hebrews* 3:8, 10, 12, 13, 18 builds up into a picture of conscious rebellion against **the living God**.

The only real way to combat this tendency is to act as a community under God – in other words not to leave each person to his/her own struggle with sin. Every day we should **encourage one another** to hold fast to our trust in God. The word translated **encourage** is a particularly strong one. It is used of military commanders inspiring and rallying their troops before battle. As we exhort one another to keep on trusting God whatever the circumstances, then we are helping one another to experience a **share in Christ** (see the above section for this expression of sharing).

10. A Sabbath-rest awaits us (4:1-11)

Following his warning about the danger of turning away from God, and the way in which an earlier generation had lost out on God's 'rest', *Hebrews* immediately goes on to hold out the promised blessing of **a Sabbath-rest for the people of God**. He is a Jewish man writing to Jewish people, and so he is able to make a 'natural' link between Psalm 95 and Genesis 2:1-3, both of which he uses in this section. The connection is that both passages are read during the Sabbath, and would reinforce each other in the minds of his readers. The Sabbath is the day of rest.

Trust and obedience are the two indispensable elements of our faith. Indeed the fundamental attitude which lies at the heart of what the Scripture calls faith is trust in God. Faith is not about knowing all the answers and being able to analyse all the doctrines without the slightest doubt or concern. It is about trusting God come what may. In verses 2 and 6 we read that this faithful and obedient attitude was missing in the lives of those who failed to experience God's rest. The same attitude is necessary for those who are genuinely to keep the Sabbath.

The rest which is enjoyed on the Sabbath by the Jewish community is seen as a foretaste of the great rest which all of God's people will enjoy in the Messianic Age. It is only by keeping the Sabbath, though, that the joy and reward of the Sabbath will be experienced. The term in verse 9 which is usually translated by **Sabbath-rest** could equally well be translated 'Sabbath keeping', and this may well have been in the mind of *Hebrews*. To resist the pressures of working to earn money for one's daily bread (4:10), to step back from one's ambition, to leave aside preoccupation with oneself and give the day to God in worship and fellowship with family and friends – in short, to keep the Sabbath, is to express one's trust in him for life here and now and for a glorious life in his nearer presence in the world to come.

The motif of keeping the Sabbath continues the reference to Moses in this chapter. It was Moses who brought down from Sinai the tablets of the Torah which included the commandment to keep the Sabbath (Exod. 20:8-11). The Sabbath was to be a day based around communal worship, and Psalm 95 was sung in the temple on the Sabbath. The method of relating Scripture to Scripture is typically Jewish at this point, and would have resonated in the hearts and minds of the readers. *Hebrews* is using the one term **rest** in different ways, exhausting its nuances in order to teach a lesson thoroughly. It is used for the sense of peace which comes to all believers when they come into relationship with God; it is used to refer to the Promised Land; and it is used in the sense of the resting from work that God did after the six days of creation.

In this section, then, we see *Hebrews* holding out three

representative generations who were concerned with God's rest. Firstly we have the generation of Moses and Joshua who could have entered the Promised Land, but didn't (3:16; 4:8). Even Joshua did not bring the people into the full rest of God (verse 8). Crucial to understanding this reference to Joshua is the fact that the name of Joshua and that of Jesus are simply variants of one another in Hebrew. They are identical in Greek. Joshua therefore merely prefigures Jesus in his mission to lead God's people into the great rest of God. Jesus is the one who has made the complete rest of God accessible to us.

Centuries after that time Psalm 95 was still holding out the promise of that rest if those listening to it would not harden their hearts. And so *Hebrews* comes to the generation of David who sang Psalm 95 in the temple but only knew the shadow of what was to come in Jesus. It was David's greater Son who fulfilled the promises of God. And then we come to the present generation of believers. The rest of God is still there to be received and enjoyed, but it could be missed yet again, and so we see *Hebrews'* pleading that they **be careful**.

Note, however, that *Hebrews* does not lapse into some kind of passive theology of cheap grace, whereby believers are absolved of all responsibility for their lives and conduct. The Sabbath is a day when no regular **work** is to be done. It is a gift of God and is to be enjoyed in God's presence and given back to him. But on the other hand there is another type of work which is still expected of believers. In verse 11 we are urged to **make every effort to enter that rest**. This is the language of spiritual and moral warfare – wrestling with temptations, crucifying the flesh, and resisting the devil. In this sense there is much hard work in being a faithful follower of Jesus.

What a comfort and inspiration it is to be assured here that there is awaiting us a Sabbath-rest. This is surely part of the Good News of the Gospel!

11. We dare not try to hide from God (4:12-13)

Whether we like it or not, the fact of the matter is that one day we will have to **give account** for our relationship to God – before God himself! *Hebrews* makes it clear that everything about our lives will be **laid bare before the eyes** of God. This term in the Greek is far from common, and its precise meaning is not easily translated by one phrase in English. It is used once in the context of a wrestler gripping his opponent in an inescapable hold: perhaps the image for us is that though we may seem to escape any reckoning with God all of our lives, the day will come when he has us in a grip which he will not let go.

It is also used in a few texts for the skinning of an animal: could this be the image of God seeing into our hearts and one day peeling off the covering to lay bare what is underneath? Finally, it is used occasionally in the context of a prisoner being led for sentencing with a dagger fixed to his throat in such a way that he had to keep his head high, and so expose his face to all who were ashamed at his behaviour and character: and so it is with us and God, in that the day will come when we have to face him and hear our sentence.

What a powerful image we have in this text! And *Hebrews* prefaces it with another strong metaphor. He says that we are **uncovered** before God. This is the literal word for being naked. It not only recalls the teaching of Jesus that 'there is nothing concealed that will not be disclosed' (Matt. 10:26), but also resonates for Jewish people with the message of the opening chapters of the Books of Moses. Adam and Eve were unaware of their nakedness until they sinned against God by eating the forbidden fruit. Their shame at being naked is a metaphor for their vulnerability before God as a result of their fall from grace.

And yet in Genesis 3:21 we read that God himself, as full

of grace as ever, made clothes to cover their physical nakedness. So it is fitting that just as at the beginning he clothed humanity, so at the end he will uncover us in order to hold us to account for our lives.

We will be examined in the light of **the word of God** and what is revealed there about God's will for our lives and his way of restoring us to himself in full fellowship. In contrast to his will and way, we prefer our own 'desires and devices', as the Book of Common Prayer has it. *Hebrews* speaks here about God judging our **thoughts and attitudes**. The first term in Greek actually covers what we might call today our emotional and instinctive nature, while the second certainly refers to our intellectual way of trying to run our lives.

God's word is like a sword which can cut through anything which tries to oppose it. It has the power of a **double-edged sword** and the finesse of a modern surgeon's scalpel. This, then, is a fairly devastating exposure of the futility of our attempts to hide from God. Far better to face up to the truths of the gospel now and turn to God than to have to face him when it is too late to put things right.

12. Jesus is the High Priest we need (4:14-16)

Chapter 4 closes with a return to the central theme of Jesus as the Jewish people's supreme High Priest. Israel's priests were set apart by God (this is the basic meaning of the Hebrew verb 'to consecrate') for a two-fold ministry. On the one hand they represented God to his people, officiating at the services of worship and teaching the word of God, and on the other hand they represented the people before God, bringing their prayers and offerings to God. This lies behind the early Christian community's decision to translate the Hebrew term for priest by the Latin word, *pontifex* – a word which actually means a builder of bridges!

Jesus is the perfect bridge-builder, being in himself God

and man. Because of his real humanity he was able to fully
sympathise with our weaknesses and our temptations. And
yet because of his divine nature he was also **without sin**. Such
is the importance of Jesus' sinlessness that *Hebrews* comes
back to it in a more explicit manner in 7:26. We shall also
return to it at that point. What is said here is that our High
Priest is now in **the heavens**, and so because we can be where
he is, we too can **approach the throne of grace**. Jesus has
returned home, and one day we shall join him there.

But we need to think carefully about the paradox that Jesus
has been tempted in every way that we have, and yet when
it came down to it he was **without sin**. The community who
received this letter in the first place needed to know that Jesus
did understand their weakness in the face of persecution and
temptation, and that he was not just a Lord for the strong and
those established in society. We today are no different in this.
Of course Jesus would not have known every possible
temptation which has come to men and women, married and
single, powerfully wealthy and disadvantaged, etc., but he
did have experience of the fundamental areas in which we are
all vulnerable.

At the risk of seeming to be merely playing with words, let
me try to express the teaching of *Hebrews* in this way. It is
not, as many Christians might put it, that Jesus was not able
to sin. If this were the case, then he could not have known
what it is to be tempted, and could not really sympathise with
us in this basic aspect of human nature. Yet *Hebrews* says
that he *is* able to sympathise with us. This is underlined by
the fact that it was spelled out earlier in *Hebrews* 2:17-18.

Therefore we need to understand it not in the sense that
Jesus was not able to sin but rather that *Jesus was able not to
sin*! Change the position of the word 'not' and you have
changed the meaning of the whole sentence. The difference
between Jesus and us is that we are *not* able to live without

sin in our lives, whereas he was able to live without sinning. He knew the power of temptation, but he was always able to overcome that power and remain holy and pure. Indeed we can say that it is precisely because Jesus knows that only he had the power to resist temptation that he really sympathises with us in our struggle with sin!

Jesus **has gone through the heavens** and is now at the Father's right hand. The ascension of Jesus is not simply a spiritual comma, as it were, marking the end of his earthly ministry before he returns to the earth. To see it in this way would be a very selfish way for us to view its significance. The resurrection and ascension were our Father's way of publicly vindicating and exalting Jesus as a result of his willing sacrifice of himself on our behalf. Israel's high priests went through the curtain into the Holy of Holies once a year on the Day of Atonement, but Jesus has, on one sufficient occasion, been brought through the barrier of death and utter spiritual alienation into the very presence of the Father.

Because of Jesus, *we* can therefore come before God's throne **with confidence**. It is likely that there is here an allusion to the situation under the older covenant, according to which only the high priests could approach the 'mercy seat' in the tabernacle and the temple. Certainly the Jewish believers who received this letter would have heard that allusion when they read this portion of the letter. It is in the presence of Jesus at the Father's right hand that we **receive mercy** to cover our sins and **find grace** to meet our times of need.

The invitation, **Let us then approach the throne of grace**, is one which we ignore or take for granted at our peril. To believe in God but not spend quality time in prayer is to say that we don't need his grace in our daily lives. It is, as one commentator has called it, 'practical atheism'. The other invitation in this passage, **let us hold firmly to the faith which we profess**, is equally important. When the circumstances of

our lives become very difficult, perhaps as a result of our
faith, then we must resist the temptation to compromise our
faith. Remember, *Hebrews* says, that the Jesus whom we
worship and serve as Lord knows our predicament and will
help us through the difficult times.

Jesus went much further for us than we will have to go for
him, and therefore we are encouraged to hold fast to our faith.
Paul says the same when he exhorts Timothy to 'Fight the
good fight of the faith ... In the sight of God ... and of Christ
Jesus, who while testifying before Pontius Pilate made the
good confession ...' (1 Tim. 6:12-13). The two invitations
here in *Hebrews* stress that we must not be afraid of the
consequences of bearing testimony to Jesus, nor need we feel
left to ourselves to cope when we do bear testimony.

We take comfort in Jesus' own words in this context:
'Whoever acknowledges me before men, I will also
acknowledge him before my Father in heaven.' (Matt. 10:32).

13. Jesus as our model of submission to God (5:1-10)

In 2:10 we discovered the great truth that Jesus' life was
somehow completed when he actually went through the horror
of the cross for our sake. The potential became actual, and so
the Lord himself was glorified. That same truth also bursts
out in this passage. Jesus **learned obedience from what he
suffered**. From what we see in the gospels, Jesus was always
obedient to his Father's will (e.g. Luke 2:49-52; John 4:34;
5:30; 6:38). Just before his arrest and the events which led
him to his death on the cross he was able to affirm this life of
obedience in prayer to his Father (John 17:4). And then he
gave up his life in obedience to his Father (Phil. 2:8).

How, then, could he learn obedience from his sufferings
when it was obedience which itself led him into those very
sufferings? Perhaps it is the case that his humanity was as
prone to doubting God's provision as ours is, and, like us, he

also learned from each evidence of God's providential grace to trust him even more in the next test of faith? We dare not forget that even at the close of his earthly life, after he had prayed his prayer to his Father that we read in John 17, he was still in need of trusting God and obeying him.

Matthew 26:36-46 is most significant for our present context. When Jesus died on the cross he really died. There was no spark of life left in him which he knew would be there before he died. That would make a mockery of his prayer in Gethsemane, and would mean that he had cheated death rather than conquered it. He cried out to God **who could save him from death**. No, he really died, knowing that he had to trust his Father to raise him from the dead – as all believers have to trust. Yet everything in his life on earth had given him the grounds for such trust and obedience. God never let him down or gave him cause to doubt. And so we too are encouraged by this to trust and obey.

It is surely Gethsemane which *Hebrews* has in mind when he refers to Jesus' **loud cries and tears**! The term used for these cries is a strong word which relates to the cries which a person emits as a result of excruciating pain or distress. It is not the usual term for emotional crying. As we have seen before in *Hebrews*, there is no experience which we can undergo which Jesus cannot understand. What is more, *Hebrews* tells us here that Jesus' prayers were heard **because of his reverent submission**. The term used here is consistently employed for 'the fear of the Lord'.

If we share that reverent fear of the Lord, and copy Jesus' attitude, then we too may learn obedience from what we suffer. John Calvin saw the importance of following Jesus' example here. In his comments on this passage he wrote: 'he did this for our benefit, to give us the instance and the pattern of his own submission.' We need to take to heart the reply of Jesus when Peter reacted against revelation that Jesus had to walk the way of suffering in order to realise his purpose and glorify God. Not only did Jesus rebuke him for a wrong attitude towards Jesus' mission, but he went on to challenge all of the disciples with the warning that they would all have to be prepared to suffer too (Matt. 16:21-28).

Also in this passage we have the first of eight references to Melchizedek in chapters 5-7. Why the focus on this mysterious figure from Genesis and the Psalms? The major treatment of Melchizedek comes in chapter 7 and so we shall defer a full analysis until then. But we can note in this passage that Psalm 110:4 is quoted in connection with the type of priesthood which Jesus embodies. Jesus is compared to this priest-king of Salem (Gen. 14:18) rather than to the Levitical order of priests. His name means 'my king is righteousness', and he was a worshipper of El Elyon, the Most High God.

For the Jewish believers who received this letter it was customary to see the lines of kings and priests as being quite separate, corresponding to descent from the tribes of Judah and Levi. We therefore note at this point that Jesus has broken the perceived mould. He is both King of Israel and her High Priest, in analogous fashion to the way in which Melchizedek was both king and priest for his people. Therefore *Hebrews* quotes Psalm 2:7, a verse acknowledged by Jewish people to refer to the King-Messiah, as well as Psalm 110:4.

This King-Priest has become **the source of eternal salvation for all who obey him**. Those who obey him, accepting him as their king, will find him to be the means of their salvation. And this brings us back to the central focus on the life and ministry of Jesus.

14. We need to become increasingly mature in our faith (5:11-6:3)

Twice in this section we are called to a **mature** life. The Greek term has to do with coming to a position where one can teach as well as learn, where one's life and wisdom are there as models for others. But these readers of the letter were **slow to learn**, and so they were slow to move to maturity. The phrase literally means 'dull of hearing', and it is often used in the sense of being downright sluggish and lacking in an appropriate sense of purpose. These believers were not living with a proper sense of zeal for the Lord and his word. Let us pray that this is not true of us!

They are still struggling with the **elementary truths** of God's word, a term which corresponds perfectly with our English expression, 'the ABCs' of a subject. We can hear some frustration in the voice of *Hebrews* as he regrets the fact that a generation which should be teaching the next generation is still in need of basic discipleship itself. This is probably related to what was presented in the previous section, where we saw that even the suffering of that generation should have been bringing them to a new level of maturity. Those who have learned through their suffering are able to teach and help others by their lives and wisdom. Let us pray that it is true of us!

Hebrews scolds them for still needing **milk** rather than **solid food**. (This is the same metaphor as used by Paul in 1 Corinthians 3:1-2.) However it would be a mistake for us to read into this some sort of spiritual elitism on the part of *Hebrews*. Solid food is not more important inherently than milk, and we are not being taught here that understanding the truths about Melchizedek etc. are more important than knowing the value of repentance, baptism, etc. Each type of food is necessary at the appropriate stage of human life, and just so should each believer grow in maturity and understanding.

Discipline is a key factor in all of this, and it is a motif to which *Hebrews* returns at the close of the letter (12:11). Here in verse 14 he relates those who can eat solid food to those

who **have trained themselves to distinguish good from evil**.
The Greek term which lies behind this translation of training
oneself is one which gives us in English the word
'gymnasium'. It is about effort and discipline, realising the
importance of the goal and setting oneself to do what is
necessary to reaching it. The mature believer knows the
importance of the word of God for producing the needed
spiritual muscles, as it were. Paraphrasing this as a challenge
to be *working out with God's word* may sound a little forced,
but it conveys something of the sense of the passage.

One other thing is worth mentioning in connection with
this distinguishing between **good and evil**. The Jewish
believers who heard these words would again have been
reminded strongly of the opening chapters of the Books of
Moses. God makes it clear that the tree of the knowledge of
good and evil is out of bounds for Adam and Eve, and that
disobeying God and eating from it will lead to death (Gen.
2:17). The serpent played on their natural hubris and deceived
them into eating from the tree, interpreting the knowing of
good and evil as meaning that they would be 'like God' (Gen.
3:5).

Hebrews teaches that the *appropriate* knowing of good and
evil for believers is not part of some desire to be like God,
able to be our own masters and mistresses, but it is part of our
desire to be like Jesus, following him in his example. We
need to discern right and wrong patterns of attitude and
behaviour in God's kingdom, and live accordingly.

Even a casual glance shows that *Hebrews* lists six issues in
6:1-2 which he regards as basic to the **elementary teachings**
which all believers need to have grasped before moving on to
more solid food. It is possible, as some have suggested, that
these six issues actually formed the backbone of the
catechetical classes of new believers in the community to
which *Hebrews* belonged. It might prove to be an interesting

exercise for a group of believers today to select which six issues or aspects of our faith they would select for a class for new believers.

The particular issues highlighted by *Hebrews* might seem straightforward enough, but a word is needed about each of them. **Repentance** is fundamental in any definition of a right relationship with God, but what are the **acts that lead to death**? Repentance means a complete change of attitude and direction in life, rejecting one's previous way of life and turning to God's way.

So the acts which lead to death might be heartlessly self-centred and immoral actions, whether of a gross or a subtle nature, a lifestyle which can only lead to the judgment of God. But they might be referring to the ritual acts and system which was the religious way of life of these Jewish people before they became believers. This could be the case especially if the letter was written to a group of Essenes who came to faith in Jesus as Israel's promised Messiah. The Essenes had their own way of faith, complete with special rituals and ceremonies, and they regarded these as clearly superior to those sanctioned and practised by the priestly leadership of the Jerusalem temple.

Faith in God is a phrase which is vague in English, but the Biblical and Hebrew concept of faith is quite clear and strong. The root word which lies behind it is one which refers to complete dependability and confidence. It is the same root for the word 'Amen' with which we are all familiar. To say 'amen' at the close of a prayer is to say that you have complete confidence in the rightness of the prayer. You are asking God to be gracious enough to establish that prayer and to make it so.

Faith, then, is not really essentially about believing doctrines about God, rather it is about having complete trust and confidence in him – whatever the situation of your life. This is not to say that holding to correct doctrines is not important, because it most clearly is, but it is to say that one's relationship with God grows and matures in the context of trust in him. Repentance takes us away from what we thought was going to bring us life but which was actually leading to death. However, it is not enough in itself, since it needs to be accompanied by the positive dimension of a trusting relationship with the living God (cf. Paul's words in Acts 20:21). For the New Testament, this life of faith is centred on the role of Jesus in coming to establish and nurture this needed relationship with the Father in heaven.

Instruction about baptisms is an intriguing phrase. The term used for baptism is certainly given in the plural here. This might imply that the teaching had to include the drawing of distinctions between the baptism of John and full baptism into Jesus, an area which could well have been confusing to new believers (see Acts 18:25; 19:1-5). This was a much more serious issue in the early generations of the community of Jesus' people than we realise today, and the references to it in Acts serve to alert us to the importance of appreciating the difference between those two baptismal experiences and confessions.

On the other hand, the phrase might more plausibly refer to the distinction which needed to be made between the various washings and immersions of Judaism and the baptism into Jesus. Note that the very same word used here for 'baptisms' is used in *Hebrews* 9:10 for 'ceremonial washings'. This is in line with Jewish linguistic practice at the time. The Torah contains many passages which teach about the need for ritual washings of different sorts within the community of the people of God. Baptism is qualitatively different again from all of these, and that needed to be grasped then – as now.

The **laying on of hands** does not at first seem to be on the same level of significance for believers as the other items on this list. For Jewish people this had more than one reference:

a person offering an animal as a substitute for his/her sins would lay hands on its head as a symbolic act of transferring guilt to the animal. It is possible that this is the meaning here, and so it would relate to teaching about Jesus' substitutionary death on behalf of believers. This would obviously place this particular issue on the same level as the others in the list.

However, it could be a reference to the symbolic gesture whereby fathers expressed the blessing of their sons. This is the least likely of the possible meanings in our passage. It could even be speaking about the symbolic act at the heart of the consecration of certain people in the community for special service (see Num. 27:18-19, 23; Deut. 34:9; 1 Tim. 4:14; 5:22; 2 Tim. 1:6). We must be careful not to dismiss this possibility as being of less importance than the others, since the issue of proper authority was – and is – of fundamental importance to the believing community if it is to grow and develop in accordance with God's will.

It is also possible, in my view, though this is not really discussed much by other commentators, that the laying on of hands was seen in a quite specific context. If the teaching on 'baptisms' does refer to the distinction between the baptisms of John and Jesus, as it were, as we mentioned above, then this might fit into that picture. In Acts 8:17 and 19:6 we read that the receiving of the Holy Spirit came after hands were laid on people. In both cases it is mentioned straight after a reference to baptism, as here in *Hebrews*. If this is right, then *Hebrews* is placing the receiving of the Holy Spirit on the same fundamental level for believers as the other issues on his basic list.

There is no difficulty with the next item which *Hebrews* highlights. Paul himself could not agree more that **the resurrection of the dead** is at the heart of our faith (see 1 Cor. 15:12-19). Indeed we might be right in surmising that the way in which Paul deals with this subject in that wonderful

15th chapter of his letter suggests that some congregations were having some problem in realising the central importance of the resurrection for our faith. This would give the context for seeing it here in *Hebrews*.

If it is true that an Essene group formed the basis of the community of believers to whom *Hebrews* was written, then it would make especial sense to include a focus on the resurrection (of the body) here. The Dead Sea Scrolls are ambiguous as to whether those Essenes in that camp at least believed in the resurrection of the body. Scholars are as yet divided on the correct interpretation of the relevant texts. It may be that they were more disposed to a belief in the immortality of the soul, and so had to be taught the centrality of the resurrection of Jesus, and his followers in due time, in the new faith.

Eternal judgment is the final matter emphasised here. Believers are never to forget that in the end we will face God as he questions us about our lives. One of the most quoted verses in *Hebrews* (9:27) underlines this very fact. At several points in the New Testament the resurrection and the final judgment are linked (e.g. John 5:26-30; Acts 17:31) in clear fashion. Some see here the twinning of a spiritual stick and carrot, as it were. The hope of the resurrection carries us forward in a positive manner in our relationship with the Lord, while the fear of judgment keeps us from giving in too easily to temptations which would lure us away from the Lord.

Whatever the case, these six dimensions of our faith are considered to be the milk of the Gospel life by *Hebrews*. They are the **foundation** of everything else. As a matter of fact, all of the six issues would have found their counterparts in the basic teaching of a student being prepared for a life of service and witness in the post-temple and post-Pharisee world of the early rabbis. Perhaps the key for these new believers was learning to leave behind what would become known as the rabbinic theology concerning those very issues – the milk, as it were – to move on to a mature understanding of the fullest significance of them in and through Jesus – the solid food?

15. We need to guard our faith (6:4-12)

Some of the most hard-hitting and far-reaching words in the New Testament are to found in this section of *Hebrews*, and so it is particularly instructive to note that only here in the letter are the recipients described as **dear friends** (verse 9). The word translated in this way is the same word which we know as 'agape love'. In John 1:14 we read that Jesus was 'full of grace and truth', and that combination of graciousness/love and truth/righteousness is necessary for any of us to be able to be genuinely used by the Lord to correct or challenge others. Therefore *Hebrews* is not trying to soften the blow of the warning that he knows he must bring, nor is he pretending that he is a better friend than he actually is. *Hebrews* is speaking straight here precisely because he *is* their very good friend and loves them.

Note also the personal care which he expresses in that he relates his challenge to **each of you** in the congregation (verse 11). This is no form letter to a faceless group of people. It is a personal letter to individual persons whom he knows and loves. As one commentator has put it, *Hebrews* was not rebuking a congregation, he was yearning over individual men and women, for that is what God himself does!

Just what is the serious concern here? Well, it is one thing if people who do not know the Lord live in accordance with other ways and rules of life, since they do not know better. They will still have to give an account before God, of course, as we see, for example, in Amos 1:3–2:3. However it is much worse when God's own people turn away from him and his ways to go their own way. This is an offence against God of

another calibre altogether, and will be severely punished, as
we see in Amos 2:4–3:2. The plaintive cry of Amos 3:2 rings
in the ears as a great source of shame. Peter says it would be
better if such people who turn away from the Lord had never
known the way of the Lord (2 Pet. 2: 20-22).

This is the issue here in *Hebrews*. How could those who
have been so close to the Lord fall away from him? And if
they do, how could they be restored to their former relationship
with the Lord? Those who belong to Jesus' family are
described as having **once been enlightened**. This metaphor
will go back to the image of Jesus as the 'light of the world'
(John 1:9; 8:12). It became a favourite among the early
believers (e.g. 2 Cor. 4:4; Eph. 1:18) as marking the difference
between them and the unbelieving world. Believers are those
who have seen the light of Jesus and who have chosen to follow
that light.

How could those who have seen the light then decide that
they prefer the darkness? To reject the light from the outset
because one prefers the darkness is one thing (see John 3:19-
21), but to experience life with the light and then to go back
to the darkness is almost inconceivable.

Believers have also **tasted the heavenly gift**. The Psalmist
implored people to taste and see that the Lord is good (Ps.
34:8), and one cannot imagine that having tasted the goodness
of God a person would turn away from that relationship. Jesus
spoke of himself as the spiritual food which we need as well
as the true light that we need (John 6:32-35, 48-51). Peter
also reflects this two-fold metaphor in his letter to the
congregation which required his help (1 Pet. 2:3, 9). *Hebrews*
does the same here with light and food. Only Jesus can satisfy
our spiritual appetite, and if we turn from him to another source
for spiritual sustenance, then we are surely in danger.

This heavenly gift which they have tasted definitely
includes **the goodness of the word of God**. One of the

recurring motifs of the whole letter is the importance of the word of God in our lives, and to have tasted its health-giving teaching about, and perspectives on, our lives is to realise how vital it is for our spiritual nourishment. To fail to spend time daily in the word of God is to court disaster in our relationship with the Lord.

Hebrews now says of believers that we have **shared in the Holy Spirit**. This term for sharing has already been used twice in chapter three for sharing in the 'heavenly calling' and in the life of the Messiah himself (see the comments in the section 3:1-6). All believers, no matter their differences, have in common the fact that they are bound together in the life and ministry of the Holy Spirit. To insult the Holy Spirit is to be guilty of a serious offence, as *Hebrews* makes clear (10:29), and as Jesus himself taught (Matt. 12:32).

It is the Holy Spirit who leads us to Jesus, convicting us of sin and bringing us the gift of faith. Therefore if we turn our backs on him, how can we return to a real relationship with Jesus?

Finally, *Hebrews* says that believers have tasted **the powers of the coming age**. The word translated 'powers' comes from the same root which gives us the English words 'dynamic' and 'dynamite'. The 'coming age' is a typically Jewish way of speaking about the kingdom of God in its fullness, or of the Messianic kingdom. No one has experienced this in its fullness yet, but we have certainly tasted it if we have known anything of Jesus and his love and power.

The strength of the dynamic powers which God makes available in his kingdom have transformed the lives of believers, and, again, we can hardly imagine that having experienced that intervening power of God anyone would be able to return to the hopeless weakness of his/her own strength.

This incredible catalogue of blessings which form the fabric of the life of a believer leaves the reader with an anxious question to be faced – what could possibly bring back to God anyone who rejected those blessings and the God who is behind them? *Hebrews* can hardly believe himself that this congregation would fall so far from grace. In verses 10-12 he encourages them to focus on the great three virtues of faith, hope and love (see 1 Cor. 13:13). Paul was able to commend the Thessalonians for their display of these virtues (1 Thess. 1:3), but *Hebrews* can only exhort his friends to this.

We too need to be on our guard to make sure that we don't **become lazy** or otherwise lose our way with God and lose our inheritance as God's people. *Hebrews* pleads with his readers to make sure that they **inherit what has been promised**. There is no vulgar doctrine of reward here by which we can lay claim to something which we have earned or deserve in any way. But there is a reiteration of the biblical promise that God's people will inherit a wonderful inheritance due to the grace of God.

Perhaps *Hebrews* was writing to people who were experiencing serious persecution for their faith, and so were considering giving up their commitment to Jesus? Maybe some had already done so, and others were being undermined by this fact? Whatever the case, he asks them all to follow the example not of those who give in under pressure but those who exhibit **faith and patience** in life's struggles.

Later on in the letter he reminds them of an earlier time when they *had* responded with faith and patience in the face of persecution (10:32-35). There again he spoke about the hope of a rich reward to come for those who persevere to the end. This may very well be the time which he has in mind here in verse 10 when he speaks about God remembering their love for him in the way that they had helped and were continuing to help God's people.

But we have to return to the vexed question of the fate of 'apostates'; those who **fall away**, and turn away from the Lord, the faith and the community of God's people. Members of that community would certainly have been exercised about this matter. *Hebrews* has already had reason to mention those who were perilously close to 'drifting away' and 'turning away' (2:1; 3:12). At this point in the letter he says that apostates are **in danger of being cursed,** and ultimately **burned.**

Though some believers have taken this as a literal reference to a burning punishment in hell, the context does not necessarily demand this interpretation. We are in the context of an agricultural metaphor in verses 7-8, so that burning the refuse and chaff from the fields and gardens would be a natural image for the worthless growths. The whole picture was probably taken from the storehouse of such images in the Hebrew Bible. Deuteronomy 29:16-28 is one example of a passage which might well have been in the mind of *Hebrews.* Following God brings blessing, but abandoning God brings destruction.

This is therefore an extremely serious section in the letter and in the New Testament as a whole. God is not to be taken for granted nor to be treated badly, since he is 'a consuming fire' (12:29), and those who work against him will be burned. Others have seen here an allusion to the parable in Isaiah 5:1-7 where we are told that if Israel fails to bear fruit for God then he will allow her to become desolate and decaying. The severity of the judgment is clear in either case.

I rather think that these two verses would also have called to mind the teachings of Jesus that on the one hand God's love is so great that he blesses both righteous and unrighteous people with rain (Matt. 5:45), and yet on the other hand that his own righteousness is such that he will separate the weeds from the crops in due course, though both have benefited from the same rain, and burn the weeds (Matt. 13:24-30). God will not be mocked!

This leads us to examine the shocking accusation which lies at the very heart of the warning given by *Hebrews*. He says that the behaviour of apostates is tantamount to **crucifying the Son of God all over again**. Clearly, this cannot be taken in a literal manner, though certain believers have tried to argue that in some mystical realm it does re-enact a crucifixion of Jesus. However *Hebrews* himself is one of the main teachers in the New Testament that Jesus' death and resurrection were once- and-for-all events. In what sense, then, can anyone crucify Jesus for a second time?

When one becomes a believer in Jesus, one's sins are forgiven because of Jesus' substitutionary death on the cross. This sacrifice is not only effective for sins committed before one's new life began in Jesus, but also covers all sins thereafter – provided that there is genuine repentance in each case, of course. Therefore we do not need him to be crucified again and again for our sins – his death atones for all our sins.

For all our sins except one, perhaps. If anyone comes into that relationship with Jesus and then walks away from it, denying its reality and efficacy, then it seems that *Hebrews* is teaching that the relationship has to start all over again. For such a person Jesus would have to be, as it were, crucified for a second time. But what a humiliation for Jesus, for the world or at least the other believers, to see that his death and resurrection were not sufficient once-and-for-all. This would break God's heart, not just his laws!

As *Hebrews* says, for Jesus this would be like **subjecting him to public disgrace**. What more negative testimony could there be than the sight of someone walking away from Jesus? Throughout the time of the Hebrew Bible we see that God will not suffer his name, and by extension his reputation, if we can use that expression of God for the moment, to be subject to dishonour and contempt. This jealousy of God for his good name is most especially prominent in the ministry of

Ezekiel, through whom God often says words like:

> It is not for your sake, O house of Israel, that I am going to do these things, but for the sake of my holy name, which you have profaned among the nations where you have gone (36:22).

It is bad enough that Israel should be abusing the blessings of God in her own life, but because it also leads to other nations concluding that after all Israel is no different from them and her God no different from theirs, then God must step in to protect his distinctive witness. In the same way, to turn away from Jesus is to bring him into terrible disrepute by making it seem as if he is no different from any other hero or god whom people follow one minute and then abandon the next.

The root of the term which is translated here as 'subjecting him to public disgrace' is also found in a most significant verse in Colossians. In Colossians 2:15 we read that when Jesus was crucified for us he thereby 'disarmed the powers and authorities', destroying their hold over us. But this was not achieved in a way that only God himself knew. Jesus 'made a public spectacle of them' in his triumph over them. So the crucifixion lovingly planned by God and entered into willingly and lovingly by Jesus made a 'public spectacle' of the powers who are opposed to God's plans, but the treating of that sacrifice with contempt subjects Jesus to 'public disgrace'.

The whole thing is so awful to contemplate that *Hebrews* says that it is **impossible** for those who treat Jesus in this way **to be brought back to repentance**. (There are three other places in the letter where *Hebrews* also refers to things which he calls 'impossible' – 6:18; 10:4; 11:6.) But saying that repentance can ever be impossible is too strong for some believers. Therefore there are those who say it is merely strong rhetoric for incredibly difficult or even unlikely. Others have offered the interpretation that it means that it would be impossible for the person to find their way back to God after such a desertion, whereas it is still possible for God to miraculously bring them back to himself.

Certain believers have even suggested that it reflects the profound hurt and sense of betrayal that the apostate's former community of faith experienced when a believer turned away from the Lord. Those were days of severe persecution against the believers, so to recant one's faith and thereby cast further pressure on the others would have been regarded as the ultimate sin. Would that community wish to see their former brother or sister back among them at a time when the persecution was over?

We can turn to similar situations in our own day and age where such things have happened and where those who betrayed their faith and often the faith community have genuinely repented, but have had to move to other regions or countries because the community would not welcome them back among them. Some interpret the *Hebrews* passage in this way, seeing the word 'impossible' as *Hebrews*, not God, speaking.

Understandable though that may be, it does not really square with an evangelical view of Scripture. There is no indication in the text that we are to take these words as being those of a person, whereas the others are to be read as if God were speaking to us. Therefore many believers take these words to mean just what they seem to say as their plain meaning – that it *is* possible for believers to completely fall away from their relationship with Jesus and lose their faith for ever.

Coming at it from a different angle altogether, many believers are simply troubled at the thought that someone who is a true believer could possibly turn away from the Lord into apostasy. Therefore they respond by claiming that anyone who does seem to have done so was never a true believer in the first place. Perhaps they started out in the right spirit, and they certainly may have heard the genuine word of God, but like the seed in Jesus' parable which fell on rocky places, the first flush of joy was short-lived, and, having no real roots in God, they fell away at the onset of trouble and persecution (Matt. 13:1-23). It is possible, as Jesus himself taught, for people to call him, 'Lord, Lord', and yet not really know or be known by him (Matt. 7:21-23).

There are therefore believers who take this passage at face value but see it all as a hypothetical warning to those who may be wondering whether or not it is worth while to hold onto their faith in Jesus when times get tough. In other words, were it *ever* to be the case that someone who had been so enlightened and had tasted the heavenly gift, etc., *did* turn his/her back on Jesus, then the result would be eternal separation from God. The function of the passage, then, would be to bring a proper sense of the fear of the Lord into people's lives – a godly warning!

In presenting the basic variety of ways in which believers down the generations have tried to understand and apply this passage, we need to consider the view that the people spoken of here are not believers who for whatever reason experience a serious period of spiritual barrenness or fall into a sinful lifestyle, bad though both of those scenarios are. Rather, so the argument goes, this passage is referring to those who come to actively oppose Jesus and the full Gospel message. Believers, in this view, in general need not overly worry about committing such a sin for which it would be impossible to be forgiven.

In much the same way, most believers interpret the teaching of Jesus in Matthew 12:22-32 about the 'unforgivable sin' to be analogous. It is taken to be referring not to spiritual lapses or dryness on the part of believers, nor even to succumbing to temptation and committing serious sin, but to becoming so hardened to God and the work of the Holy Spirit that even when the Lord is clearly at work the person is able to attribute it to the devil – God's active opponent.

All in all, then, this is a hard section of the letter, and at the very least it should serve as a warning to us not to take God or our walk with him for granted. *Hebrews* is so concerned that apostasy might infect the community that he warns against it in three other passages in the letter – 3:12-19; 10:26-31; and 12:25-29. We need to show **diligence to the very end**. We must not **become lazy**. We must **imitate** the **faith and patience** of others who can serve as role models for us.

16. We can trust God's promise (6:13-20)

In all of this concern for our determination to persevere and keep moving on with Jesus it is also vital that we don't lose sight of the fact that God is faithful, and that ultimately we depend on his mercy and grace, not our own commitment and love.

Abraham is brought into our minds again as an example of the kind of person we are to imitate. Even although God's promise to Sarah and himself of a great family of descendants must have seemed ridiculous, he had faith in God and he waited patiently. And the day came when he **received what was promised**. *Hebrews* returns to this watershed of faith in chapter 11:11-12.

Yet the focus is on the fact that God made and kept his promise to Abraham. God has the initiative in all relationships, and we are indebted to him for deigning to make any promises to us. *Hebrews* now points out something of great significance in the case of God's relationship with Abraham. The word of God is sufficient in and of itself to be trusted, but God went as far as sealing his word with an **oath**. Not that it was necessary, but God thereby gave *double* assurance that he could be trusted. His word is his bond, but he gave a bonded oath as well.

That promise given at the call of Abram (Gen. 12:1-3) was ultimately fulfilled in Jesus, Abraham's greatest descendant. Indeed we can go further, and say that in Jesus all who follow him also inherit the life of blessing promised to Abraham and his descendants. Therefore in the context of the previous section, *Hebrews* is quite intentionally going on to reassure his brothers and sisters that their hope for God's blessing at the end of the period of persecution will be rewarded because God can be trusted.

This hope that God will look after his people is described as **an anchor for the soul**, an image which fast became one of the best loved in the community of believers. It is found from very early times as a visual symbol on the gravestones of believers and on various works of Christian art. We can rely on our hope when other emotions and experiences threaten to wash us away into a sea of chaos or onto rocks of despair. The biblical definition of hope is not of a wishy-washy feeling which is nothing more than an inability to face reality. It is of a **firm and secure** trust that God cannot be defeated and that his purposes will also therefore prevail. It is positive and healthy, changing lives and creating a people who will serve God with courage and calmness.

Mixing the metaphor somewhat, *Hebrews* goes on to say that our hope can even take us into **the inner sanctuary behind the curtain** which separated the Holy of Holies from the rest of the Jerusalem temple. Jesus made that journey **on our behalf** and we can now enter that most sacred space with him. We know that once a year only could one man only – the high priest – enter that place to enact the ritual of the Day of Atonement. Jesus has opened up that place – representing the very presence of God himself – for all believers. This, of course, is the awesome event which lay behind the tearing down of the curtain in the temple when Jesus died on the cross. What is more, it was torn from the top, not from the bottom, showing us God's hand at work in this (Matt. 27:50-51). Our hope that one day we shall actually stand in the nearer presence of God is a sure one.

When Jesus is described here as the one who **went before us**, the term so translated is a lovely one. At its simplest level it meant someone who runs on ahead of others, much as a child might innocently do on a walk with his/her parents. But it then came to be used in a more particular sense for someone sent out in front of the main party to act as a sort of scout and troubleshooter. Jesus went ahead of us through death not merely in a chronological sense, but in the sense that he made it possible for us to follow him. As Jesus said to his disciples, he had to go ahead to prepare a place for them (John 14:1-3). He has already fought the battles on our behalf, and he has already prepared a place for each of us in our Father's house.

17. Melchizedek, the royal priest (7:1-10)

This chapter of the letter is dominated by the figure of **Melchizedek**, and *Hebrews* is quite clear that he is of fundamental importance to us as we seek to understand the type of High Priest Jesus is. But Melchizedek is an obscure character as far as any biblical presentation is concerned. He was presumably a person of considerable influence and power, but the minimal reference in Scripture only gives us clues to that importance (Gen. 14:18-20).

The bare bones of that incident are that Abram, while returning from a successful military campaign against certain Canaanite kings, is met by another king, called Melchizedek. He offers bread and wine to Abram, thereby acknowledging his victory, praises God for that victory, and asks God to bless Abram. In passing we can note that *Hebrews* does not refer to the offering of bread and wine, even though it seems to us that it would have been an obviously relevant aspect of the whole incident. Abram's response is to accept Melchizedek's authority and then offer him a tithe of the battle prize.

Melchizedek then disappears from the historical narrative of the Hebrew Bible. He comes and goes suddenly. The only other mention of him in the Hebrew Bible is in Psalm 110:4, a highly significant Messianic Psalm which *Hebrews* quotes later in this chapter. The Psalm was already seeing a typological value in Melchizedek, and *Hebrews* teases out the full significance of this typology. There are several clear areas in which Jesus is presented as relating to Melchizedek.

Melchizedek was a **priest**, appointed by God as a bridge-builder between God and people. This priestly ministry is basic to the life and work of Jesus, as *Hebrews* is at pains to make clear. But Melchizedek was also a **king**, having royal authority over his subjects. Jesus is also a king, and indeed is Lord of all the earth as well as the legitimate and ultimate King of the Jewish people. If we ask why *Hebrews* could not simply have used Aaron and David as two great role models for priest and king out of the history of Israel, then the answer that *Hebrews* would give is that Melchizedek was brought into the picture by God to show us how someone could be both priest and king – a clue, as it were, that when the Messiah came he would be a priest-king.

However this actually raises a potentially serious problem regarding the Messiah. In many cultures there is no difficulty in having priest-kings, and they exist. But for Israel the problem was that God had already decreed that her priests would be descended from the tribe of Levi whereas the rightful king would be a descendant of the tribe of Judah. Since no-one could be descended from both tribes, this would seem to disqualify any priest-king for Israel. Here before us is the significance of the figure of Melchizedek, whom we learn was the priestly head of the succession to which Jesus belonged. Jesus is the son of David, from the tribe of Judah,

thus satisfying the royal requirement. However, he does not
receive his priestly credentials from the tribe of Levi, and so
it is no crisis that he is not a Levite. He is a priest **in the order
of Melchizedek.**

What else do we know about this person? His name, as
Hebrews points out, means **king of righteousness.** Therefore
he also represents righteous authority, a virtue brought to
fulfilment in Jesus. He was the **king of Salem**, and both the
likely derivation of the name and the parallelism of Psalm
76:2 suggest that this was the place known in Scripture as
Jerusalem. The term 'salem' is probably derived from the same
root as the familiar Hebrew word, 'shalom'. Indeed the name
'Jerusalem' itself might well be a phrase meaning 'city of
peace'. Therefore Melchizedek also represents a rule
characterised by peace, again fulfilled in the reign of Jesus.

One of the most famous and important of the Messianic
prophecies in the Hebrew Bible establishes the vital relationship between these two facets of the Messiah's character and
reign. In Isaiah 9:6-7 we read that the Messiah will be known
as the 'Prince of Peace', and that he will 'reign on David's
throne ... with justice and righteousness'. Melchizedek is relevant in this context.

At this point *Hebrews* introduces another important analogy
between Melchizedek and Jesus, but it is one which leaves
many believers today less than persuaded as to its legitimacy.
In the passage in Genesis where we meet Melchizedek we are
not told anything about his ancestors or immediate family.
Given the seriousness with which genealogies are treated in
Genesis, and the startling importance of this man in Abraham's
life, this is perhaps a little surprising. It is all the more
surprising since Israel defined a priest's authority in terms of
his lineage (from Aaron's family within the tribe of Levi),
and given the significance of Melchizedek's role as a priest,
his family line would have been of the utmost importance.

Genesis does not say that he had no parents, etc., but as far as
the text goes, there is no actual record. *Hebrews* sees major
significance in this lack of a genealogy.

That significance is compounded by the fact that we are
not told of the death of Melchizedek either. He really is a
mystery as he suddenly appears and disappears in the text.
Hebrews interprets it all by saying that Melchizedek is
presented to us as a man **without beginning of days or end
of life**. In this respect he also reminds us of Jesus! Jesus had
no human father, and in fact he existed eternally before his
birth as a human being. And Jesus will certainly live for ever.
Hebrews is using a Jewish method of interpreting Scripture
known as midrash, which is perfectly respectable in the Jewish
community to whom the letter was written. He can imagine
Melchizedek as an eternal priest, appearing at strategic
moments to do God's bidding, and this speaks of Jesus, who
is certainly **a priest for ever**.

Abraham was certainly convinced of the authority of
Melchizedek. For all Abraham's undoubted greatness in the
history of Israel – its physical and spiritual father – he accepted
the blessing of Melchizedek and offered him tithes. *Hebrews*
underlines the shock experienced by Jewish people reading
this by spelling out that **the lesser person is blessed by the
greater**. Abraham, the father of the faithful, therefore had
less authority than the king of Salem, a non-Israelite.

On a particular point, we learn from Scripture that the
descendants of Levi were the ones to collect tithes from the
other Israelites. Yet in this case the Levites, descended from
Abraham, and therefore, figuratively speaking, represented
by Abraham, actually *gave* tithes to another person – and a
non-Israelite at that! Melchizedek was surely a powerfully
important person. When we give this more thought we see
that there is yet one more surprise to come. The Levites had a
right to ask for tithes because the Lord had given them that

right and expressed it in the Torah. But Melchizedek had no
national or spiritual relationship with Abraham, and yet he
seems to have had a personal, charismatic authority which
led Abraham to *offer* him a tithe. This suggests a priesthood
of a high order indeed.

As *Hebrews* says when pondering the significance of
Melchizedek: **just think how great he was**.

18. Melchizedek points forward to Jesus (7:11-19)

Once again we meet the Greek root for reaching a goal or for
becoming completed, although it is often translated by the
English term **perfection**. The goal which was in mind for the
priesthood was the establishing of complete reconciliation
between God and Israel. This is only possible in and through
Jesus, our great High Priest. Jewish people would be inclined
to respond that the priestly system initiated in the Torah can
effect that reconciliation, so *Hebrews* takes some time to
explain why this is not so.

He states that this goal of complete reconciliation could
not have been **attained through the Levitical priesthood** –
otherwise why would God have sent Jesus to be our High
Priest? *Hebrews* has in mind the promise given in Psalm 110:4
to which he has made allusion earlier. This verse in this
Messianic Psalm speaks of an order of priesthood which would
have been thoroughly inappropriate had the Levitical order
been sufficient for Israel's needs. We shall return to this point
in the next section of the letter.

Hebrews then sets out the Levitical priesthood, by which a
person becomes a priest not on the basis of character or gifting,
but simply **on the basis of a regulation as to his ancestry**. If
your ancestor was Gershon, from the tribe of Levi, then you
were a priest. If your ancestor was Gershon's great-grandson,
Aaron, then you could be the high priest of Israel. In contrast,

Jesus is High Priest **on the basis of the power of an indestructible life**. Jesus himself is the one who has the authority and power to effect our forgiveness and reconciliation to God. The promise in Psalm 110 was a word to us that such a priest **in the order of Melchizedek** would have to come to deal with the problem of alienation from God, since the Levitical priesthood could not do it.

Even more fundamentally, that provision of priestly help for the time before Jesus came was based on the Torah, which itself was unable to realise fulfilment of the goal of reconciliation. As *Hebrews* says, **the law made nothing perfect**. In the same way, Paul taught in one of his letters that the Torah was unable to make anyone into a righteous person – it serves in another fashion altogether by showing us how sinful we are. As he puts it, 'through the law we become conscious of sin' (Rom. 3:20).

Although we must be careful not to despise the Torah, since it was clearly God's gracious communication of his will to Israel, and as such is still called 'holy' and 'spiritual' by Paul even after his coming to faith in Jesus (Rom. 7:12, 14), in *ultimate* terms it could only produce a priesthood which was **weak and useless**. It had nothing in itself which could empower change in people, and such a claim was never made for the Torah in the Hebrew Bible. It served as a tutor to convict us of our sins, to lead us to appreciate and confess our distance from God, and to make us realise our desperate need for *God* to somehow solve the problem of our lives.

Jesus is the one who has the power to change us. In fact, *Hebrews* says, the Torah was so inadequate in itself that *it* had to be changed. The change of order of priesthood for the Messiah, from Aaron to Melchizedek, implied **a change of the law**. Jesus as High Priest was not, as might have been expected by the Jewish people who followed him, defined by nor confined to the Levitical order of priesthood. He came with **a better hope**, making it really possible for us to **draw near to God**.

19. Jesus is an eternal priest (7:20-25)

Psalm 110:4 is finally quoted in the section of the letter which reverberates with the importance of that verse. *Hebrews* brings our attention to the fact that the Psalm teaches us that God **has sworn** about the significance of this Melchizedek order of priesthood. The Levitical priests and Aaronic high priests all came into their office without any special promise or oath being sworn by the Lord. However, Jesus **became a priest with an oath**. There is something new and unique about Jesus, so outstanding that God himself seals Jesus' ministry with his own oath.

Hebrews expresses this in what is one of the most consistent and characteristic insights in the whole letter – he says that God's personal promise of this new priesthood means that the covenant enacted by Jesus is **a better covenant** than what went before. We first met this emphasis on Jesus and everything about him being 'better' or 'superior' in *Hebrews* 1:4 (see the first two sections in this commentary). We will return to it in chapter 8 where it has some prominence.

At this point it will help to underline the pastoral concern of *Hebrews* for the congregation to whom he wrote his letter. He was distressed at the thought that some might back away from the difficulties of life as a believer in Jesus and settle for a life which was in every way a distant second best. How could he let them fall back into a life which was going nowhere?

Jesus has brought a 'better hope', based right now in **a better covenant** which was in turn based on 'better promises'. Jesus' death on our behalf was a much 'better sacrifice'. Without trying to minimise the seriousness of the persecution which many of them had faced, as a result of which some had lost their homes and livelihoods, it was nevertheless true that they had before them, if they stayed with Jesus, a 'better possession'. As long as they were true to Jesus, they were sure of life in a 'better country'. It was 'a better resurrection' that they saw in front of them. (*Heb.* 7:19, 22; 8:6; 9:23; 10:34; 11:16, 35)

Putting it succinctly, life with Jesus is incomparably better than life without him!

Hebrews moves on now to present another facet of the superior nature of Jesus' priesthood. Picking up from the verse in Psalm 110 which he quotes here, *Hebrews* points out three times in the chapter that Jesus is **a priest for ever** (7:3, 17, 21). In contrast to every other priest, Jesus' ministry is eternal – death cannot put an end to him or his ministry. It may be that some of these believers were so anxious, as a result of their experience of persecution, that they were beginning to wonder whether Jesus was really as able to help them now as when he walked the streets of Jerusalem and the fields of Galilee (2:3-4).

Hebrews assures them that Jesus' priesthood is **permanent**. The Greek term here comes from a legal context, being used of decisions and principles which are absolute and which cannot be taken from their rightful source and claimed by anyone or anything else. Therefore Jesus' ministry on our behalf cannot be taken from him or claimed by anyone else or by any other system.

Jesus **lives for ever**, offering his help at every turn. The Greek root used here is not the regular word for being alive, and in fact it is usually translated by the verb 'to remain'. Therefore it does not simply mean that Jesus will not die. This particular root carries with it a sense of service. We find it in contexts where a person has to remain in service to someone until a debt is repaid, etc. When the service is fully paid, then the person is free from the responsibility of remaining and can move on.

It seems therefore that there may well be here an indication that Jesus not only lives for ever, but also lives to serve us for ever. His responsibility to us will never end. It is not that he has to repay a debt to us, since he owes us nothing. On the contrary, we owe *him* our lives, a debt which can never be repaid. No, but because of his great love for us, he lives to act as a servant to us. Jesus' own words shame us as we realise that Jesus, the *Lord* whom we are called and privileged to serve, and yet whom we serve so poorly and reluctantly, has committed himself to serving us:

> For even the Son of Man did not come to be served, but to serve, and to give his life as a ransom for many (Mark 10:45).

Jesus is **able to save completely** all those who acknowledge him as their High Priest – which is to say those **who come to God through him**. No supplement of any kind is needed. The Greek tense of the verb **to save** is the present tense, thus emphasising that he is always able, in any given moment of need, to save his people. This 'complete' saving of his people is summed up by *Hebrews* as Jesus living for ever with a commitment **to intercede** for them.

Thereby he nurtures and sustains us day by day. This becomes the more significant when we realise that one of the ministries which the rabbis accorded to the angels was that of intercession on behalf of Israel. Jesus is the one who knows us, understands us, loves us and can actually make the difference to us – not the angels. In the light of the role the angels played in the life of those Jewish believers before they came to faith in Jesus, it was obviously extremely important for *Hebrews* to leave them in no doubt about the identity of the great intercessor (see also Rom. 8:34).

Finally, let us note that Jesus is the **guarantee** of this new covenant relationship with God. The Greek term used is found only here in the New Testament. It is one used of a person who offers himself as security for the repayment of a loan, or for the appearance of someone who is on bail at the court. We can take what might seem like a risk because the Jesus whom we meet in the gospels and in the lives of believers is trustworthy. He can be taken at his word.

If anyone wishes to know what God is really like, then he/she can study the life and teaching of Jesus and find out.

20. Jesus is spiritually and morally pure (7:26-28)

He is the High Priest who really **meets our need** – he is **holy**. This is not the Greek word which signifies being set apart for God's purposes, but another term, which carries with it the sense of faithful duty to God and complete devotion to his ways. It is used of overseers over the congregations (Titus 1:8), and of all those who wish to come before the Lord in prayer (1 Tim. 2:8). Jesus is the person who personifies this radical commitment to God's ways.

He is also described as **blameless**, a term which actually conveys the idea that he was completely without evil influence in his life. There is only good in Jesus – and so much so that his life can act as a barrier to wickedness. More than this, Jesus is described as **pure**. This was a term which could be used of ritual cleanliness, since it means to be free from blemish or defilement of any kind. Sacrificial animals had to be without any blemish to be worthy of presentation before God. Unique among us, there was nothing about Jesus which would have prevented him from coming into God's presence.

In this sense he certainly was **set apart from sinners**. However, we must beware letting this subtly affect us into thinking that Jesus was somehow not really human at all. Nothing could be further from the truth, and throughout

Hebrews we are being constantly reminded of Jesus' wonderful humanity. The difference with Jesus was that, unlike us, he was able not to sin (a truth we looked at in the section 4:14-16). He lived his life fully in the Father's presence, yet all the while loving us and making it possible for *us* to come into the Father's presence.

Hebrews continues his praise of Jesus by stressing that he is now **exalted above the heavens**. Once again we see that *Hebrews* is determined to press home that the angels are not worth comparing with Jesus, who is far above them. Presumably *Hebrews* is thinking here of the ascension of Jesus, by which he was exalted by his Father to sit at the Father's right hand. This perfect person, Jesus our Saviour, is now sitting at the right hand of God.

Hebrews now points out yet another way in which Jesus is superior to any other high priest. Each year, on the Day of Atonement, the high priest had to offer a sacrifice for his own sins before he could offer any sacrifices on behalf of the people of God. The sinner had to confess his own sins before daring to speak of the sins of others. In complete contrast, Jesus had no sins to confess.

The Levitical priesthood could only produce and sanction high priests **who are weak**, but God's promised High Priest, his own Son, has been made **perfect for ever**. His sacrifice only needed to be offered **once for all** on our behalf.

21. Jesus serves in the heavenly tabernacle (8:1-5)

When *Hebrews* speaks here about Jesus at God's right hand in the highest heaven, he uses a word to refer to God which stresses his transcendence. He calls him **the Majesty**. This is a typically Jewish way of referring to the awesome greatness of God by not actually using the term 'God' at all, but substituting another term. To this day Orthodox Jewish people

will most frequently refer to God by the expression 'HaShem'.
Many Christians are familiar with the traditional words for
thanking God in the Jewish community: 'Baruch HaShem'.
It means, 'Blessed be the Name!'

The Hebrew word 'HaShem' simply means 'The Name'.
God is The Name above all other names that could be given –
and this is the context in which to appreciate the significance
of Paul's teaching about Jesus that

> God exalted him to the highest place
> and gave him the name that is above every name (Phil. 2:9).

God is so great that our language just serves to limit our
understanding of him as well as helping us to speak about
him at all. So the Jewish community uses various expressions
to refer to him in language which draws attention to our
inadequacy of ability to define him. The term used here in
Hebrews is one of those expressions. God is the very ideal
and personification of majesty.

But we should also note that *Hebrews* is reminding us that
for all of the majesty of Jesus – and *Hebrews* emphasises in
many ways the glory and perfection of Jesus – he is still **at
the right hand of the throne of the Majesty in heaven**, rather
than being 'the Majesty' himself. In other words, God the
Father has the final authority in the relationship of the Trinity.
The Son is not the Father, and does not try to usurp the Father's
place.

Since Jesus continues to serve us in heaven at our Father's
side, interceding for us, and with his sacrifice of himself
continuing to be effective on our behalf, *Hebrews* sees this in
terms of him continuing to act as a priest. He presents Jesus
as a High Priest who continues to serve in a sanctuary. But in
this case the sanctuary is really worthy of Jesus. It is **the true
tabernacle** which was **set up by the Lord** himself, not by
inadequate and sinful people.

The sanctuary on earth serves only as **a copy and shadow** of the 'true tabernacle' in heaven. The point being made is not that we are to imagine Jesus literally moving about in a sanctuary area in heaven, since his ministry is clearly not of a physical nature. Rather, the point is that in comparison with the efficacy of Jesus' once and for all sacrifice while he was here on earth, and the power of his intercessory ministry in heaven, anything else is feeble and can only serve as a pointer to Jesus and the need for Jesus.

Many commentators on *Hebrews* have tried to insist that the background thinking here is not Jewish at all, but Platonic. This is not a reference to platonic relationships, meaning friendships with no romantic entanglements, but to one of the basic pillars of Plato's philosophy of life. Plato taught that there are two distinct levels of reality in life, only one of which is truly 'real' and of any genuine worth. This is the spiritual or heavenly level – the realm of 'ideas' and 'perfect forms'. Everything in the physical universe is a mere copy or reflection of its perfect 'idea'.

According to this Hellenistic worldview, everything on earth is simply a poor copy or shadow of the ideal world of spirit and idea. It is obviously a system of thought which looks similar to the presentation which we find here in *Hebrews*. But we are not working with that Platonic view here. This is good Jewish and Hebrew thought in *Hebrews*. He is not supposing an image of the perfect sanctuary in heaven, but he is exalting the ministry of Jesus in spiritual language and metaphor.

The word translated by **copy** is one which means a sketch or outline plan. The word behind the translation **shadow** means exactly that. Both terms refer to something which gives a good and helpful indication of the real thing, but something which in itself is insubstantial. They are no substitute for the real thing.

Therefore what we are being shown is that the priestly and sacrificial system which God inaugurated for the people of Israel was a needed and helpful indicator of the type of ministry which is really needed and efficacious. But in itself that system was not sufficient. Nonetheless it was necessary in its time to prepare God's people for an understanding of what is really needed for our salvation. Therefore the whole cult system had to be enacted just as God directed. **Moses was warned** by God to see to it that his instructions were followed completely, in order to ensure that the proper guidelines were being set down for Israel.

22. Jesus and the New Covenant (8:6-13)

In any list of the most important issues in the Bible, that of 'covenant' would be one of those at the very top. When God chooses a person or a people for his purposes (what the Bible calls 'election') and actually establishes a relationship with them, the highest form of relationship is called a covenant. The covenant which God made with Israel forms the background to this passage in *Hebrews*.

The Hebrew word for covenant and the cultural context out of which it came both fit perfectly with the way in which we see the relationship between God and Israel being defined in the Bible. It was not a contract between two equal parties with both sides receiving equal benefits. This type of covenant was a relationship between a person (in this case, God) with superior power or authority and another party. The senior party offered protection and a sense of belonging to the weaker party, and in return the lesser party offered loyalty and service to the stronger.

Even though the two parties in a covenant were not equal, there was still a mutuality of sorts in a covenant relationship, and we know of several in the ancient near east between

nations. When God committed himself to a relationship with
Israel, he chose this as the model to be used. God pledged
himself to care for and protect Israel, and Israel committed
herself to God as her only Lord and God. There were always
stipulations about behaviour in these covenants, and of course
we see the same in the covenant relationship between God
and Israel.

God could – and would – discipline Israel if she ever broke
the laws of the covenant, whether in terms of considering other
gods or in terms of immoral behaviour. What is wonderful
about God's commitment to Israel is that even though he
promised that he would punish Israel severely if she ever
needed it, he also promised that he would never abandon her
nor break his covenant relationship. Time after time in the
Hebrew Bible we see occasions when God could have given
up on Israel in the light of her attitudes and behaviour. Yet he
never did.

It must have broken God's heart to see the fickle nature of
Israel's love for him and for one another. But rather than walk
away from the relationship, God promised that a new covenant
relationship would one day be established within the context
of the existing one. This is the covenant to which *Hebrews*
refers. Jesus made it possible for that new covenant to be
realised. A full study of the covenant brings home the
wonderful grace of God. We can spoil our relationship with
him, and we can go as far as to lose his blessings in our lives,
but we cannot stop God loving us and wanting our restoration.
Jesus personifies that love of God.

There is a common Greek term for agreements and contracts
between people, but in the New Testament we discover that a
different term from this is used for God's covenant with his
people. The term used is one which most commonly is used
for wills. A will is not a mutual agreement, but an expression
of the 'will' of the testator. He/she sets the 'conditions' and

the actual 'blessings'. Those who are mentioned in the will can only accept or decline to accept whatever is offered.

God has generously decided to offer us life and blessings, and our part is to receive or reject. This is the heart of the Good News. It is therefore no coincidence that the compilers of the part of the Bible which follows on from the life of Jesus called it the 'New Testament'. We still use in English the term 'last will and testament'. The word 'testament' simply comes from the Latin term which translates the Hebrew and Greek words for 'covenant'. New Testament is just another way of saying New Covenant.

Before going on to analyse this a little more in the context of the *Hebrews* passage in front of us, it would be helpful to pause for a moment to realise that this same type of covenant commitment from God forms the basis of the Church's relationship to God. All Christians can and do break the laws of the kingdom of God and grieve the Holy Spirit, but that in itself will not turn God against us. His grace and commitment to us is astonishing.

A major question which Christians need to address is why so many Christians over the generations have been content to assume that God would abandon Israel for her constant disobedience and sins in spite of his pledge to an everlasting covenant with her. And yet those same Christians also assume that God's pledge to the Church will never be broken – even though the Church's record of disobedience and sin is just as great. The biblical account seems clear enough. God has not written off the Jewish people.

This does not mean that it does not matter whether Jewish people accept Jesus as Israel's Messiah and Lord or not. The New Testament is clear that God's plan is for Israel to believe in Jesus and to take this Good News out to the Gentiles. Salvation is only found in Jesus. And this brings us back again to the matter of God's plan for the salvation of Israel within the context of his covenant commitment. The actual promise of the new covenant relationship is found in Jeremiah 31:31-34, and *Hebrews* quotes that passage here.

Jesus is the **mediator** of this new covenant. The Greek term here comes from a root which means to be in the middle, and suggests someone who stands in the middle and acts as a link between parties on either side. The same term is used in the famous passage where Job laments that he has no such mediator to link him to God, who seems to have withdrawn from Job (Job 9:33). Jesus is therefore the one who acts as the bridge, or link, between God and ourselves. In this case, he makes possible a new covenant relationship.

But this Greek term can also be used to denote someone who stands between two persons or groups who are in dispute with one another. The mediator acts as a peace broker, or a reconciler. This meaning fits perfectly with the situation before us. As we said above, God had to do something to deal with the constant breaking of the covenant by his people. God certainly had cause for dispute with Israel and the whole world. Jesus is the one who effected reconciliation. The importance of this matter is seen in the fact that Jesus is called mediator again in *Hebrews* 9:15 and 12:24 (see also 1 Tim. 2:5 for the same term).

So what was *new* about this covenant? First of all *Hebrews* reminds his readers that Jesus had not invented this himself. The newness did not consist in it being created out of the blue. It was already promised by Jeremiah. In fact he goes on to stress that Jeremiah's promised new covenant underlines the inadequacy of the existing covenant relationship. Otherwise, **no place would have been sought for another**.

But it is not the case that the old covenant itself was flawed in terms of its content or intent. Although verse 7 here does say that something was **wrong with that first covenant**, verse 8 goes on immediately to say that **God found fault with the**

people. The 'flaw', or inadequacy of that covenant lay in the fact that it could not change the people. The people **did not remain faithful** to that covenant. What was needed was a new covenant *relationship* between God and his people. Paul knew this to be true, as we see from his testimony in Romans:

> the law is holy, and the commandment is holy, righteous and good ... We know that the law is spiritual; but I am unspiritual ... (see Rom. 7:7-25).

When Jeremiah spoke of a new covenant he simply used the Hebrew term for 'new'. It is a term which is capable of various nuances, such as 'renewed', and this may well be what was intended. However in Greek there are two words for 'new'. One of them just refers to chronological time – something is old in time and something else is new. The other word, which is the one used here, carries with it the sense of new in quality or kind. For all of the fact that this new covenant was promised long ago, and was therefore expected at some point, there is nevertheless a real sense in which it was of a nature which far surpassed any expectations. This particular word for 'new' reinforces the comparison between the two covenant relationships which is expressed in the words of Jeremiah's promise: **it will not be like the covenant** which God made before at Mount Sinai.

What, then, happens to the older covenant in the light of this new one? *Hebrews* says that it is **ageing**, and that it **will soon disappear**. The former word gives the sense of decaying and fading away. The second word is even stronger, meaning to be abolished or wiped out of existence. The same serious language is used by Paul in 2 Corinthians 3:7-18. This cannot mean that the old covenant, which *God* put into place, was useless or tainted by sin. In the same way, the old system of priesthood, also established at *God's* command, was a good thing in itself. But the old covenant was only ever there for a season – until the time came for the coming of the Messiah and the new covenant (see Gal. 4:4).

The radically new dimension of this new covenant therefore encompasses its new mediator. Jesus, though the expected Messiah, was not predictable. There was no blueprint in the Hebrew Bible which people could simply read in order to create the Messiah. He is, as the Son of God, transcendent and sovereignly free. No one was ready for Jesus in the fullest sense.

Because of the coming of Jesus, God will be able to heal the first terrible schism in the history of the people of God – that between the tribes of Israel after the death of Solomon. The ten northern tribes split away from the Davidic monarchy and the capital city, Jerusalem, forming the nation thereafter known as 'Israel'. This left the other two tribes to form the nation called 'Judah' (see 1 Kgs. 12). This break within the people of God was bad enough, but at one point relations between the two groups became so bad that there was even a civil war (see Isa. 7).

God promised to heal that schism as part of the new covenant, since it broke his heart as much as the other sinful attitudes and behaviour of the Jewish people. So we read that the new covenant will be **with the house of Israel and with the house of Judah**. This message of healing within the Jewish people may also be what lies behind the words of John 11:51-52 where we read that Jesus would not only die for 'the Jewish nation', but also for 'the scattered children of God'.

The story of the 'lost tribes of Israel' is commonly known. This refers back to the historical fact that the northern kingdom of Israel fell to her enemies (the Assyrians) well over a century before the fall of Jerusalem (at the hands of the Babylonians). The historical fate of those ten northern tribes is much disputed, but certainly many of those people were moved and kept moving further east and north. Thereafter, the Jewish

Diaspora was an accepted reality of life, for all that it represented a quite unacceptable break in the family of God. The reference in John 11 is probably to the Jewish people living in the land of Israel and those in the Diaspora.

This promise not only brings Good News to the Jewish people but also points to the fundamental ministry of Jesus in reconciling all people to one another in his love for them. He alone can unite Jewish and non-Jewish people under a covenant relationship with God, and bring about the blessing which was already a major part of God's original covenant with Abram (see Gen. 12:3b; Rom. 11:17-24; Eph. 2:14-21). Jesus alone can effect the truly godly relationship between different people (see Gal. 3:26-29).

Even within the renewed people of God there will be a new maturity in relationship with God which will transform other relationships. Every one of them will **know the Lord ... from the least of them to the greatest**. Once again we can see here a promise which reaches beyond the Jewish people to embrace the whole world. In Isaiah we read the promise that the day will come when 'the earth will be full of the knowledge of the LORD as the waters cover the sea' (Isa. 11:9; see also Hab. 2:14). People from every nation will be able to know the Lord for themselves, so that Jewish neighbours will no longer need to tell their Gentile neighbours to know the living God (see John 10:16; 1 John 2:2).

This marvellous vision of such a relationship with the Lord presupposes a radical and profound desire to obey him, since it is impossible to know God unless we are obeying him. As John wrote:

We know that we have come to know him if we obey his commands. The man who says, 'I know him,' but does not do what he commands is a liar, and the truth is not in him. But if anyone obeys his word, God's love is truly made complete in him (1 John 2:3-5).

The trouble with the old covenant was that the people of Israel **did not remain faithful** to it. Therefore, as an integral part of the reality of the new covenant, God promises that he will find a way to ensure that his people follow him from the desire of their own hearts rather than simply out of a sense of duty or fear. This is what God means by saying: **I will put my laws in their minds and write them on their hearts**. This had always been the goal of God's covenant, as we see in passages like Deuteronomy 6:6-9, where God says to the Israelites that the commandments of God 'are to be upon your hearts' (see also Ezek. 11:19-20; 36:25-28).

Once again we see how this would be so significant for the Jewish believers to whom this letter was written. In patriarchal times, there was a ceremony which was a necessary part of the making of a covenant. An animal would be sacrificed, since every transaction in those cultures was religious in nature, and then its carcass would be split in two pieces. These pieces would be set up on rocks or pillars and the parties to the covenant would walk between them. This apparently acted as a kind of self-imposed curse whereby the parties declared that if they broke the terms of the covenant then they would also deserve death.

It is vital that we notice that when God made his covenant with Abram, a similar ceremony was part of its ratification. In Genesis 15 we read that God instructed Abram to kill several animals which he then cut in two and arranged appropriately. But at the crucial moment God sent Abram into a deep sleep, so that he was not able to walk between the pieces of the animals. While he slept, God appeared in the form of fire, and 'passed between the pieces'.

In other words, God was indicating quite clearly that this was an unconditional covenant. He alone was its guarantor. This did not mean that Abram/Abraham and his descendants could live as they pleased *vis-à-vis* God and others, but it was the great enacted promise that God was *absolutely* committed to the covenant relationship. Such is the grace of God.

But the grace of God is about to take his people by surprise once again! According to this new covenant relationship, God is going to become the sole guarantor in an even more radical sense. Not only will he continue to be merciful and forgiving when others would have given up on the other party, but he will now change the very hearts of his people so that they now have a genuine commitment to love, serve and know him. Because of our dependence on the work of God in our hearts to make it possible for us to fulfil our part of the covenant, it is almost as if God is now committing himself to taking on *both* sides of the covenant stipulations.

The more we come to know God, the more we come to appreciate the distance between him and us. And yet the more we come to appreciate the wonder of his love. Knowing God involves knowing our need for forgiveness and a growing joy at the realisation of his capacity to forgive. Central to the new covenant, then, is the promise of forgiveness and a completely new start for those who come into that new relationship with God. When people come to God in Jesus, God promises that he **will remember their sins no more.** Sin is not a disqualification for entry into the kingdom of God!

At Passover time the Jewish community celebrates the great work of God on their behalf when he redeemed them from Egypt in the days of Moses. Following that act of deliverance God led them to Mount Sinai where he made them into his people with the giving of the covenant. It was at a Passover celebration that Jesus led his disciples into the mystery of the new covenant, dependent on the act of deliverance which Jesus accomplished on the cross. He said, 'This cup is the new covenant in my blood' (Luke 22:20).

This new covenant is the basis for our relationship with God, and *Hebrews* gives us plenty of food for thought as we reflect on it.

23. The earthly tabernacle and true worship (9:1-10)

Hebrews speaks here about the splendour and impressiveness of the tabernacle, which served as the focal point of worship for the Israelites under Moses' leadership and the covenant which he mediated. Such a reminder of the **earthly sanctuary** would not only be more powerful for those Jewish believers whose heritage it was than it is for most Christians today (at least in the western traditions), but it would be even more poignant if this letter was written after the destruction of the second temple in 70 AD.

That tabernacle and its sacred furniture still holds an indelible place in the psyche of Jewish people. In fact there are many Christian traditions which accord a significant place to the tabernacle, viewing it in allegorical terms. We see in the design set out in Exodus 25-31 and 35-40 that the original tabernacle was really just a glorified tent patterned after the classic bedouin-type tent of the prevailing culture. A family's tent would open up to visitors and spill out onto rugs on the ground in front of it. Then you would enter the tent proper, as it were, which is to say the main living quarters. Off to the side, behind a heavy veil, was the women's quarters, a place of special honour and protection.

When we turn to the tabernacle, and to the temple for that matter – the dwelling places of God among his people – there was an outer 'court', which acted as a buffer zone, as it were, between the everyday world and the sanctified space of the Lord's special presence. From this court you entered the **Holy Place**, with its special furniture and ambiance. Then, at the heart of the sacred space, lay the **Most Holy Place**. This was the place where only the high priest could venture, and that only on the Day of Atonement. We shall return to this shortly.

The very concept of a sacred space is obviously one which God used to help his people come to realise that worshipping God is not an activity which can be entered into without thought or preparation. There were penalties for treating the tabernacle lightly and wandering into its precincts by accident or carelessness. The physicality of the tabernacle (and later the temple) was a useful aid to understanding that the 'otherness' of God is vital for us to grasp. And yet at the same time, God is present with us in a way which can be taken for granted or missed.

The tabernacle was a tent made out of materials which the Israelites knew, found and fashioned. It did not drop out of heaven, made out of materials not found on the earth. That would be the stuff of science fiction stories. So it might have been possible to take it for granted. God often works in clearly supernatural ways in our lives, but usually he is at work every day in ways which we might take for granted. To see the tabernacle was to be reminded of the Lord and his presence.

This symbolic function must not be undervalued. It was God's plan, and it worked. Of course our human tendency to sin meant that it *was* possible for people to take the Lord for granted. The physicality of the tabernacle and temple was misunderstood by some to imply that God's presence was guaranteed whatever their lives and worship were like. The sacred space was almost held to have power in itself to protect and bless.

But the truth of the matter is that only the Lord is holy in himself. Everyone and everything else is holy only in association with the Lord. He sanctifies us by setting us apart for his service, and in that way we can be called 'holy'. So the ground around the burning bush was holy because the Lord was there, not because it had inherent holiness. The tabernacle had a **Holy Place** because of the Lord's presence and purpose. Without the Lord's presence and blessing a holy structure, piece of furniture, geographical place or person will be just a building, etc.

This was the reason for Jeremiah's distress when the people

took their confidence from the presence of the temple, assuming that it guaranteed the Lord's presence.

> Hear the word of the LORD, all you people of Judah who come through these gates to worship the LORD. This is what the LORD Almighty, the God of Israel, says: Reform your ways and your actions, and I will let you live in this place. Do not trust in deceptive words and say, 'This is the temple of the LORD, the temple of the LORD, the temple of the LORD!' If you really change your ways ... then I will let you live in this place ... (Jer. 7:2-7).

At best, however, the tabernacle and temple served the purpose of pointing to the presence of the Lord and to the need to take worship seriously. It must have been a glorious sight and experience to enter it. And the furniture was also splendid and impressive. In the holy place stood a great **lampstand**. The Hebrew term for this is 'menorah', and this is a commonly known word in the English language. It was made of gold and had seven branches coming from a central stem. Each branch ended in an oil lamp for lighting. It survives as one of the most potent symbols of Judaism and the Jewish people. The metaphor of light in the darkness is an obvious one for the presence of God with his people.

In the same area stood **the table and the consecrated bread**. This was an acacia-wood table covered in gold which held the loaves of bread which represented the tribes of Israel. The bread was restricted for use by the priests, and was freshly made for each Sabbath (see here Matt. 12:1-8). The metaphor of the Lord as the provider of food for his people is another evident one.

Also in this area, but close to the curtain which marked the Most Holy Place, stood **the golden altar of incense**. For most of the year this was used by priests in their daily duties of offering incense as well as the other sacrifices. But on the Day of Atonement, which is the focus of *Hebrews* in this section of his letter, the high priest took a golden censer of coals from this altar into the Most Holy Place (see Lev. 16:12). This is what is in *Hebrews'* mind at this point. The incense symbolises the prayers of the people ascending to God, as we see expressed in Revelation 5:8; 8:3-4.

The area where these two pieces of furniture stood was behind a curtain which screened it from outside view. Behind a **second curtain** was the area which housed a piece of furniture of incomparable significance – **the gold-covered ark of the covenant**. Above all else this represented the mercy and presence of God. It was a chest which contained reminders of the miraculous way that God had preserved his people in the period of wandering in the wilderness with the tabernacle.

In it was **the gold jar of manna**, speaking of the way in which God kept the people of Israel alive and nourished during that forty-year time of discipline (Exod. 16:33). During the annual feast of Tabernacles the Jewish people to this day celebrate the protection and blessing which God gave them in that generation. The joy of it is that the wilderness time was one of severe punishment for Israel's rebellion and lack of gratitude to God. In other words, even when God needs to discipline his people he still cares for them and will protect them. This is the measure of God's grace.

The ark also contained **Aaron's rod that had budded**. This refers to the dead staff of Aaron which miraculously 'budded, blossomed and produced almonds' as clear evidence that Moses and Aaron were God's chosen leaders for the people in that wilderness period (Num. 17:10). God never leaves his people without leadership which reflects his own authority.

Finally, there were in the ark **the stone tablets of the covenant**. Moses brought these down from Mount Sinai, and they represented the revelation of God to his people. There in that desert region of Sinai he spoke to his people and set the course of history. But even more wonderful is the fact that after Moses received the stone tablets from God and the people offended the Lord by the sin of the Golden Calf, the Lord gave them a new set of stone tablets (Exod. 32-34). The first set were destroyed in an expression of Moses' anger, but the Lord then immediately put that anger in context by instructing Moses to make a second set.

Reinforcing the fact that God's anger with his people comes out of a deeply loving commitment to them, a love which must step in to discipline where necessary (see Prov. 3:11-12), and not from a fickle nature, the Lord makes the point by saying to Moses at that time that he is:

> The LORD, the LORD, the compassionate and gracious God, slow to anger, abounding in love and faithfulness, maintaining love to thousands, and forgiving wickedness, rebellion and sin. Yet he does not leave the guilty unpunished ... (Exod. 34:6-7).

Above the ark were **the cherubim of the Glory** (see Exod. 25:18-22; 37:7-9). It was cherubim who guarded the Garden of Eden on God's behalf (Gen. 3:24). It would also seem that God chose to manifest himself between the representations of the cherubim when he met with and spoke with Moses in the tabernacle (Exod. 25:22; Num. 7:89). In fact we often find references to God's 'presence' between the cherubim (see 1 Sam. 4:4; Pss. 80:1; 99:1; Isa. 37:16; Ezek. 10:1-5).

The Hebrew term for 'presence' which became a somewhat mystical name for the presence of God is 'shekinah'. This vitally important word comes from the same Hebrew root which gives the word for the tabernacle – mishkan (the root letters in both words are sh k n). The root has to do with settling or dwelling. The tabernacle was the place where God symbolised his dwelling with Israel, and the shekinah was the presence of God settling over his people.

That term, shekinah, is regularly translated into English as 'glory'. Hence the fuller expression here in *Hebrews* for the cherubim. This is the only place in the New Testament which mentions them, though they are found in over 90 references in the Hebrew Bible. They were winged creatures, but little is known of their character or appearance. They served as guards and servants of God's presence on earth.

These cherubim, according to *Hebrews*, overshadowed **the place of atonement**. This phrase refers to the 'mercy seat', as it is called in some translations, this being a way of emphasising that here was the symbolic seat of God's mercy. From here the Lord expressed his forgiveness of his people on the Day of Atonement (Lev. 16:2). The Greek word which is used in the Greek translation of the Hebrew Bible for the lid of the ark, the mercy seat, as it were, is only used twice in the New Testament.

One of those two occurrences is here in *Hebrews*, speaking of the place of atonement under the old covenant. The other verse is in Romans, relating to Jesus himself as the ultimate place to turn for mercy (Rom. 3:25). And this, of course, is the insight of *Hebrews* – to help us to see that all of the good aspects of the faith of Israel finally serve to point us to Jesus. He personifies all of the spiritual values and principles of the tabernacle and temple.

The beauty of the old way fades before the beauty of Jesus. In verses 6-10 we are told explicitly that the old way was flawed by its inadequacies and limitations. Jesus suffers from neither. The old ways were good and great in their time, and must not be despised, but ultimately they are **only a matter of ... external regulations** when compared with the life that Jesus brings.

Paul discerned the very same truth, and put it in his characteristically blunt way:

> If anyone else thinks he has reasons to put confidence in the flesh, I have more.... But... compared to the surpassing greatness of knowing Christ Jesus my Lord... I consider them rubbish... (Phil. 3: 4-8).

24. Jesus' death is more powerful than any sacrifice (9:11-15)

The words used here for **redemption** and **ransom** both come from a root which gives us one of the richest metaphors in the Bible. This Greek root comes from the language of the slave market, referring to the buying into liberation of a slave. The image is rooted in the language of the Hebrew Bible (see Lev. 25:48; Num. 18:16; Pss. 111:9; 130:7).

By using this language *Hebrews* underlines the central truth of the New Testament that Jesus has become the new Lord of the life of everyone who follows him and is called by his name. As we have come to understand life, each of us has a Lord who is overseeing our lives and to whom we are accountable, whether we are aware of this or not. Those who do not belong to Jesus are under the rule of the devil. They are slaves to the devil, to sin and to their own selfish nature. *Hebrews* is teaching us that Jesus sets us free from the devil's rule so that we are no longer the devil's slaves.

But what happens at a slave market? Someone else comes along and buys the slave from his/her previous owner. The slave is still a slave. And so it is with us when Jesus frees us from the power of sin and death – he now becomes our new Lord. Paul's favourite description of himself is as Jesus' slave, as we see, for example in Romans:

Paul, a servant [literally a bond-slave] of Christ Jesus, called to be an apostle and set apart for the gospel of God (Rom. 1:1).

It is expressed most clearly for us in the following passage:

You are not your own; you were bought at a price (1 Cor. 6:19-20).

So although we are **set free from sins**, we are not set free to be our own masters or mistresses. This is further re-enforced in *Hebrews* by his statement that the purpose of this new life which Jesus makes possible is **so that we may serve the living God**. Ours is to be a life of service to God. The Greek term used here is one which speaks of total surrender, and it is often used in the particular sense of duty to God and worship of him.

Indeed the whole concept of 'the service of God' in the Jewish context, expressed through the very vocabulary of the Hebrew Bible, is bound up with the concept of 'worshipping God'. The basic Hebrew term for 'worship' is also the very word for 'work' or 'service'. This does *not* mean that worshipping God was seen as a chore or merely a legal requirement, as some have tried to imply. What it means is that all service done for God, including having an attitude to one's daily work that it too should be done to please God, is a way of offering him our worship. The Bible does not accept the facile difference between the sacred and the secular. All of life is of concern to God, and he wishes to be Lord of every aspect of our lives.

What it also means is that worshipping God is not something which we should do only when we feel like it. God is worthy of our worship – our awe, adoration and surrender – even in difficult times. It is part of the service which we owe him. The very same Hebrew root gives us the word for a 'servant or slave'. Such a person is bound to serve his master in every situation of life. Paul's favourite description of himself was as a 'bond-servant of Jesus, the Messiah' (see, e.g. Rom. 1:1), and those who call Jesus 'Lord' must realise that they are thereby calling themselves his servants.

This terribly important point about worship/service of God as being our duty, as it were, as well as our delight, is beautifully expressed in the word used by *Hebrews* to refer to those who love and serve the Lord. He speaks about **those**

who are called to this relationship. The term used here for 'calling' is used in Greek of invitations to weddings and parties (see Matt. 22:3; Luke 14:8; John 2:2), therefore the sense of delight and honour. But the same term is used of a 'summons' to appear in a court, and therefore we have the sense of obligation and accountability.

Worship is far more than praise! It refers to the surrender of our whole life to God and the commitment to serve him in every situation of life. We have been cleansed of sin **so that we may serve the living God**.

Hebrews then repeats from the previous section that Jesus served God as High Priest in a **more perfect tabernacle** than the one built by the Israelites, acceptable though that one was to God. Many Christians over the generations have actually believed that this better tabernacle is a reference to Jesus' own body. When the Israelites went into the tabernacle they were coming into the special presence of God. In the same way, when people came to Jesus they met with the greatest ever expression of the presence of God (John 14:9).

Jesus' self-sacrifice was also incomparably greater than that of the two greatest sacrificial events in Israel's life. People could only be made **outwardly clean** by means of the sacrifices of the old system. What were these two pinnacles of Israel's cult?

Firstly, *Hebrews* speaks about **the blood of goats and bulls**. This is likely to be a reference to the rituals of the Day of Atonement. This was the annual day of national repentance. The high priest sacrificed a bull for his own sins, something Jesus did not need to do (Lev. 16:11). He then sacrificed a goat for the sins of the people (Lev. 16:15). Unique to that day, he took another goat, known as the scapegoat, and symbolically transferred the people's sins to its own life. He then sent it out into the wilderness to die there (Lev. 16:21-22).

This day was bigger than any other day on which many people might have been offering sacrifices for their sins – it was the day on which God covered over the sins of the whole nation for the preceding year. But it was still of less than absolute value and effectiveness.

Hebrews then speaks about **the ashes of a heifer** being used to cleanse people. The reference here is to the powerful cleansing effect of a flawless red heifer which we read about in Numbers 19. Only this remedy could deal with the impurity which came from contact with a dead body. An unblemished red heifer was killed outside of the Israelite camp, and the ashes from its burned carcass were mixed with cedar wood, some hyssop and a piece of red material. The resulting watery mixture was what was sprinkled on a person to render them clean once again. Note that this is the only case where the death was ordered to take place outside of the camp.

One of the greatest of the medieval Jewish rabbis, Maimonides, actually taught that the high priest was also sprinkled with this watery mixture before he went into the Most Holy Place on the Day of Atonement, reinforcing the need for purity in that place. This is a traditional teaching, but it would make sense of its inclusion at this point of the letter. On the other hand, this cleansing agent was so important in the life of the community that it would merit inclusion in its own right.

Whatever the case, *Hebrews* is emphasising that these sacrifices could not touch our soul and really change us. They could deal with ritual defilement and the Torah's requirements, but only Jesus' death could set people free from sin. In short, only Jesus could go beyond helping us to acknowledge and do something about our sins to actually bringing **eternal redemption** – rescuing us from the power of sin.

This chapter of *Hebrews* really pushes home the contrast between the old and **new covenant.** The old tabernacle doesn't compare with the new one (9:1-5, 11, 24). The external effectiveness of the old rituals doesn't compare with Jesus' internal and eternal effectiveness (9:9-10, 12-14). The temporary nature of the old sacrifices doesn't compare with the permanent nature of Jesus' death (9:25-26; see 10:3).

It can all be summed up in one way by saying that only Jesus can free us **from acts that lead to death**. Although this phrase may refer to sins of all sorts in our lives, since sin does lead to death, it is perhaps more likely in this context that it refers to the attempts which we make to deal with our sins. Ritual acts in themselves have no power to bring redemption – not even the ritual acts of Israel which were in fact ordained by God for his people. They played their part in Israel's life, acting as catalysts and symbolic enactments, but they were never going to be enough in themselves. As Paul says about the whole Torah in Galatians, the rituals were simply a 'school teacher' given by God 'to lead us to the Messiah' (Gal. 3:24).

Finally, in this section, it is worth noting that in verse 14 we find a lovely allusion to the Father, the Son and the Holy Spirit. The Messiah, through the Spirit, offered himself to the Father. And so we are at last able to **serve the living God**.

25. Without the shedding of blood there is no forgiveness (9:16-22)

Let's begin by looking at the last verse in this passage. The Torah lays down that almost everything of significance in Israel's past relationship with God had to be **cleansed with blood**. Blood was one of the most potent of the symbols in Israel's life, and we see its importance in passages like Exodus 29-30 and Leviticus 1-9, 14-17. It is clear that blood is saying something about both life and death. This is the basic issue facing all of us, and *Hebrews* climaxes this particular passage with teaching about the fundamental nature of our need for the **shedding of blood**.

However we should note that *Hebrews* draws our attention to the fact that it is only **nearly everything** which needs to be so cleansed. Ritual uncleanness could sometimes be dealt with ritually just by the symbolism of 'water' (see for example Lev. 15:5-11). But of course Jesus also knew the significance of this powerful symbol, and referred to himself as the source of the water of life (see John 4:7-15; 7:37-39). Another potent symbol was 'fire', and we see this in effect in Numbers 31:22-23.

But if the issue was the need for forgiveness of sins, then only blood could serve as the effective agent, since **without the shedding of blood there is no forgiveness**. At this point it is necessary for us to think about the meaning of the blood sacrifices. There are two options open to us as we seek to understand the theological impact of blood. Was it perceived essentially as a symbol for life or death?

In Leviticus 17:11 we read as follows:

> For the life of a creature is in the blood, and I have given it to you to make atonement for yourselves on the altar; it is the blood that makes atonement for one's life.

Sacrificing an animal and therefore 'releasing its blood', so to speak, could have been seen primarily as releasing life. This in turn would have carried the symbolism of new life becoming available for the person making the sacrifice. Many Christians work with this interpretation of the need for blood sacrifice. Jesus' crucifixion would therefore be seen as a giving of his life for us, indicative of the fact that he does indeed give us life (see John 10:10b).

Others, however, see the blood sacrifices as focusing on death. The death of the animal acts as a reminder to the person bringing the sacrifice that he/she might be in danger of the same fate, and he/she benefits from the death and the shedding of blood. Christians who work with this basic understanding see Jesus' crucifixion as his substitutionary death for us.

Hebrews emphasises that under the Mosaic covenant **the scroll and all the people** were sprinkled with blood, as were **the tabernacle and everything used in its ceremonies** (see Exod. 24:1-8; Lev. 8:15-19). This sprinkling was also part of the ritual on the Day of Atonement, as Hebrews states (see Lev. 16:14-16). The reason for this was that until something was associated with sacrificial blood it was not considered pure or fit for God's purposes. Hebrews is telling us that this was a pointer to Jesus himself, and that it is Jesus' death on the cross which makes atonement, purity and service of God possible.

We began at the concluding part of this section in Hebrews because its climactic words are so fundamental to New Testament teaching about Jesus. Blood is central to the process of atonement, and the shedding of blood in a full sacrifice necessarily involves the death of the sacrificial animal. In Jesus' case it involved his death on the cross. Thinking about death suggested another powerful image to Hebrews, and it is with this thought that he opened this section of the letter.

The word used in Hebrews and in the rest of the New Testament for **covenant** was the one used in everyday Greek for a will or a legacy. So in verse 16 we find a rather bold and creative play on words in order to make a valid and important point. When he wrote to them, **In the case of a will**, he might actually have written, 'In the case of a covenant'. The point which he makes is this: just as a *will* only comes into effect on the death of the testator, so too the *covenant* could only become effective on the death of Jesus.

Everything is potentially obtainable while the person with the gifts is alive, and it may even be known what the inheritance is going to be, but those gifts are only to be inherited in fact when the giver has died. In the case of believers in Jesus, the covenant brings 'the promised eternal inheritance' (verse 15). For the covenants of Noah, Abraham and Moses there was the death of the sacrificial animals (Gen. 8:20; 9:9; 15:9, 17-18; Exod. 24:1-8). These animals died, symbolically, on behalf of those receiving the honour of such a covenant relationship with God. With the new covenant it is Jesus who died on our behalf.

26. The purpose of Jesus' return (9:23-28)

In this section of the letter we come across one of the characteristic expressions of *Hebrews*. His joy in the life and death of Jesus is bound up with his appreciation of the fact that Jesus' work of atonement was done **once for all**. There is no need to repeat Jesus' sacrifice of himself, and this makes it unique. The Greek term for **once** is actually used twice in this section, stressing its importance (verses 26, 28).

This teaching is reinforced by the use of a tense in Greek for the verb **to take away** sins which itself implies an action which happened only once. We can do nothing to help in our own atonement – it is entirely the work of God. We can only thank him for his grace and commitment to us.

But on the other hand, there is nothing which we can do to make it necessary for Jesus to go through it all again. Notwithstanding the teaching of *Hebrews* 6:6, the objective fact is that Jesus' death on the cross was sufficient for all time. I still need to repent of the sins which I commit day after day, and I need to acknowledge my need for the daily efficacy of Jesus' death on my behalf, but the power of sin has been dealt with once and for all. No sin can necessitate a repeat of the cross. This is also a wonderful testimony to the grace and faithfulness of God.

Hebrews uses two rich metaphors to help us to understand what Jesus has done for us in freeing us from the power of sin. Firstly, he presents a legal context. The verb in the phrase

to do away with sin is a legal term meaning 'to annul'. It is the same verb used in *Hebrews* 7:18 for 'setting aside' the former covenant regulations. This means that sin has no longer any claim to us – even though we don't need much persuasion sometimes to act as though it did.

How often have we prayed in the words of the Lord's Prayer that he will not lead us into temptation, and then sooner or later walked into temptation all by ourselves! We must be more careful in the way we lead our own lives under God, but the fact of sin in our lives does not mean that God has not dealt with the fundamental problem. The devil has no right to our lives when we belong to Jesus, our new Lord, and any claim he might have tried to make has been 'annulled' by the Lord.

This is the teaching of Paul in Romans, when he spells out the same point:

> When you were slaves to sin, you were free from the control of righteousness ... But now that you have been set free from sin and have become slaves to God, the benefit you reap leads to holiness, and the result is eternal life (Rom. 6:20-22).

Secondly, *Hebrews* presents a priestly context. The verb in the phrase **to take away the sins** is used very often in the Greek translation of the Hebrew Bible (Septuagint) to describe the actions of the priests in bringing the sacrificial victim to the altar. Jesus is seen here as the (willing) victim who receives, as it were, the sin of the world upon himself. This is also emphasised by Paul in his letter to the Corinthians:

> God made him who had no sin to be sin for us, so that in him we might become the righteousness of God (2 Cor. 5:21).

It is also likely that *Hebrews* is specifically echoing the words of Isaiah 53:12, the climactic words of that great prophecy of the 'Suffering Servant'. Isaiah concludes his chapter with

words which include these: 'For he bore the sin of many'.
Hebrews says in verse 28 that Jesus came **to bear the sins of
many people**. The verb in *Hebrews* can be translated by 'to
bear' or 'to take away'. The whole prophecy of Isaiah 52:13–
53:12 is an appropriate and moving meditation for this section
of the letter of *Hebrews*.

At this point, however, we need to acknowledge that
although the cross has dealt with the power of sin once and
for all, the world is far from being free from the influence of
sin. The devil is still active, and he is still having 'success'.
Hebrews is well aware of this reality, and as we have seen, he
faces it in 2:8-9 where he writes:

> Yet at present we do not see everything subject to him. But we see
> Jesus ...

If we press that phrase, 'at present', then we could infer that
the time will come when the situation will change once and
for all. In the present section of *Hebrews* we see that such an
inference is indeed correct! Jesus will return one day to
complete the process which has irrevocably begun with his
first coming to earth.

In verses 26 and 28 we see the following dynamic
presented: **But now he has appeared ... to do away with sin
... and he will appear a second time, not to bear sin, but to
bring salvation**. I think that it is likely that Bruce and others
are right in suggesting that *Hebrews* has the ceremonies of
the Day of Atonement still in mind at this point. On that Day
the high priest entered the Most Holy Place on behalf of the
people. Tension would have been extremely high and the
outcome uncertain until he returned into view from behind
the curtain to confirm that all was well.

Just so, Jesus is presented as having ascended into heaven,
to the absolutely Most Holy Place. One day he too will return
into public view to confirm and proclaim the promised

salvation. Paul teaches explicitly that 'not all who are descended from Israel are Israel' (Rom. 9:6), and so *Hebrews* speaks about only **those who are waiting for him** as the ones who can be confident of salvation.

We should now take a look at the central importance in the New Testament of this teaching about Jesus' return. It does not always receive the attention which it should in today's churches, but it is fundamentally significant for the Christian faith. Jesus' return is frequently spoken about in the New Testament, clearly taught and consistently applied from the teaching of Jesus himself right through to the last writing in the Bible.

There are different interpretations in our churches concerning the timing of Jesus' return, the nature of the signs which will accompany it, etc., but it is not our brief to go over all of that in this commentary. However, the fact and purpose of that return should not be neglected here. There are five major reasons given in the New Testament to explain its central importance.

When Jesus returns he will bring about the final defeat of the devil and his forces (1 Cor. 15:24-26).

When Jesus returns he will bring about the final judgment of the world (1 Cor. 4:5).

When Jesus returns, as it says in our passage here at verse 28, he will complete the redemption of the redeemed (1 John 3:2; 1 Thess. 4:16-17).

When Jesus returns history will reach its climax and fulfilment (Rom. 8:19; 2 Pet. 3:13; Rev. 21:1).

When Jesus returns he will at last receive the public vindication and honour which have been denied him for so long (Mark 14:62; Phil. 2:6-11; Rev. 1:7).

Hebrews says here, in effect, that the full experience of **salvation** is yet to come. This in no way dilutes the reality of the fact of our salvation here and now, but it is an acknowledgment of what we all know to be true – namely that the devil is still active and our own self-centred natures are still very much struggling for control of our lives. The fulfilment is still before us, and we are earnestly **waiting for him** to return so that we can finally rest in him.

27. Jesus' self-sacrifice was once and for all (10:1-18)

Hebrews gives us a recapitulation here of what could be seen as the heart of the message of the book. The Torah is described as being **only a shadow of the good things that are coming**. The word for 'shadow' means a pale reflection or a meagre outline, lacking full definition and substance. It is a good guide, but no substitute for the real thing.

We are then told that the Torah does not constitute **the realities themselves** to which it points. The actual Greek phrase which lies behind this translation says that the Torah is 'not itself the image' of those 'good things'. The word for 'image' in the phrase means an exact reproduction or representation. It was used to describe a perfect portrait of someone. Therefore *Hebrews* is saying that the Torah is not the *absolute* word of God – only Jesus is!

It should, however, be pointed out at once that this does not mean that *Hebrews* had a poor view of the Torah. Many Christians have tried to present this as the New Testament teaching – namely that the Torah was and is useless and a hindrance to God's work. We have already seen that this is not the teaching of Jesus or the authors of the New Testament books. With regard to the system of sacrifices, the specific focus here in *Hebrews*, we read in verse 8 that it was not just a human system, and consequently of no value. **The law required them to be made.**

It is *in comparison with* Jesus that we see the severe limitations of the Torah, but the Torah in itself is still God's good gift to his people. It will be helpful to repeat here the words of Paul when he agrees with *Hebrews* that Jesus and not the Torah is the perfect revelation of God. Paul puts it like this:

> I consider everything a loss compared to the surpassing greatness of knowing Christ Jesus my Lord, for whose sake I have lost all things. I consider them rubbish, that I may gain Christ and be found in him ... (Phil. 3:8-9).

Notice that the focus is on the comparison. Without the pointer to Jesus many would not have found him; without the outline of Jesus many would not have recognised him; without the shadow of Jesus many would not have realised that he was there at all. But once having found Jesus himself, everything else pales and receives its proper, lowlier, place.

Hebrews lays bare an obvious truth, that the very need to repeat the old sacrifices was proof enough that they were not really effective in themselves. They were right for their time, since God himself instituted their place in Israel's life, but their function was to continually draw attention to the fact that sin was serious and had to be dealt with. Repentance and a heart which wanted to serve God was always a necessary dimension of the cultic acts.

Hebrews states that the Day of Atonement itself, the most awesome of the rituals of sacrifice, really only served as **an annual reminder of sins**. As the Day came round the people would become more conscious of the enormity of the gulf between themselves and their holy God. This in fact is still true today among pious Orthodox Jewish people. But this is also a purposeful and positive service when blessed by God. Being conscious of the barrier of sin and the need to have it dealt with can in itself lead people to cry out to God for mercy.

This in turn can lead to a conviction that faith in Jesus' atoning death is the only way to really deal with the problem of sin.

In another context, Paul also helps us to realise this spiritual dynamic that *if God is in control of the process* then even grief or guilt, etc. can be transformed into a life-changing experience for the better. In his context he puts it like this:

> Godly sorrow brings repentance that leads to salvation and leaves no regret, but worldly sorrow brings death (2 Cor. 7:10).

Martin Luther grasped this dynamic of the function of the Torah very well, and it is still a mainstay of Lutheran theology. Even the Sermon on the Mount, he argued, is to be seen in this way. As we read it and realise that living in accordance with its challenge to us is impossible for us to live out, so we are compelled within ourselves to fall down before the Lord to confess our need for his grace to enable us to live in this way. We also realise our need for his forgiveness when we fail.

It is the consistent testimony of those whom we sometimes call 'saints' – those believers who really walk close to the Lord and serve as much loved role models for others – that the closer they walk with Jesus the more they are aware of how far short they fall of God's standards. They are more aware of sin in their own lives and in the world around us than are most Christians. The Torah serves as our teacher and our guiding shadow.

Reflecting the context of *Hebrews* as a letter dealing with the priestly nature of Jesus' life and work, not least because his audience was particularly influenced by these considerations, we see that in contrast with Paul's emphasis on the issue of justification, being made right with God, *Hebrews* is concerned with the issues of purification and sanctification. Therefore we see his focus reflected in his teaching that because of Jesus' life and death **we have been**

made holy. While we wait for the return of Jesus to complete the process of our sanctification he describes us as **those who are being made holy**.

This means being 'set apart' for effective service and worship of God. The sacrifice of Jesus has made this a real possibility for Jew and Gentile alike. His sacrifice was 'once and for all', and we might be allowed to make a play on words in that English translation. Jesus died once, and this is effective for all time. But Jesus' death on that one occasion is also effective for all people. *Hebrews* expresses this beautifully by referring again to Psalm 110:1 in relation to Jesus and in contrast with all other high priests in Israel. The unique efficacy of Jesus' death is symbolised by the fact that afterwards Jesus **sat down at the right hand of God**. There was no need for any other action.

It may be of interest to point out that the religiously-oriented Jewish communities today are finding different ways to cope with living without the repeated sacrifices. They do not accept Jesus' death as offering atonement, and in fact they do not expect the Messiah to fulfil that function when he comes. The Jewish religious authorities ruled long ago that in the absence of the temple and the sacrificial cult God would accept substitutes for the sacrifices. The rabbis spoke of a dispensation, as it were, for the Jewish people to live without cultic atonement until the temple is rebuilt.

As they say, it was not the Jewish people's decision to live without a temple, and it is only the nations' hostility to the Jewish people and the degeneration into secularism among many Jewish people today which is preventing the rebuilding of the temple in Jerusalem.

The Jewish Prayer Book has been designed to reflect the temple services, and when Jewish people pray in the synagogue they are, in effect, echoing and substituting for the liturgy of the temple. Repentance is still seen as a prerequisite for forgiveness, and alongside this, regular prayer and giving generously to charity make up the trio of attitudes and actions which replace the sacrifices in this time without the temple.

Orthodox Jews, then, are awaiting the coming of the Messiah (not Jesus) and the rebuilding of the temple with consequent restoration of the priestly service and the sacrificial cult. In the meantime substitutionary methods are accepted for the forgiveness of sins. On the Day of Atonement many Orthodox Jewish men will kill a cockerel and swing it over their heads and the heads of their family members with appropriate words of prayer in a symbolic sacrificial act. Even more symbolically, an increasing number of Orthodox Jewish men don't even kill the cockerel. They swing it above their heads with the same prayers, but then give it away to an impoverished family to eat as a family meal.

The Reform and Conservative Jewish communities do not share in the Orthodox expectation of a Messiah and a temple. For them, the sacrificial cult is a thing of the past, useful in its day but with no place in today's society. They do accept the traditional substitute of repentance, prayer and charity, and see them as the permanent substitution. So much is this the case that they have even developed the tradition of calling their synagogues 'temples', indicating that they see the synagogue as the new centre of Jewish spiritual life. There is no new temple to come.

Christians and Messianic Jewish believers differ on whether or not the temple will be rebuilt in Jerusalem, or whether Jesus is meant to be acknowledged as the new temple of God on earth (Matt. 12:6). There are also different interpretations of the purpose that such a temple would have in God's economy for the Messianic Age. But our agreement is far more important – that the loss of sacrifices and priests in the temple is no loss at all as far as our salvation is concerned.

Jesus' once and for all death on the cross is the sufficient atonement for the world.

There is one other matter which must be looked at in this section of the letter. In verses 5-7 we are presented with what is a quote from Psalm 40:6-8, but a comparison of the Psalm with *Hebrews* shows immediately that even allowing for the slight inconsistencies of translation there is a significant difference between them. The second half of Psalm 40:6 reads, 'but my ears you have pierced/opened' and the supposed quote reads, **but a body you prepared for me**.

This divergence from the Hebrew text is explained by the fact that it is a quotation from the Greek version of the Hebrew Bible – the Septuagint. We have already had cause to discuss this version (pages 19-21), and it seems clear that *Hebrews* used it often. Indeed he might have been much more fluent in Greek than in Hebrew for all that he was a Jewish leader. That was a sign of those times.

The important thing for us to note is that the essential meaning of the two lines is the same. According to the Hebrew we have the metaphor of 'opening' someone's ears so that he can hear better, and by extension obey more easily. The Hebrew could also be translated as 'piercing' the ear, thereby referring to the ceremony of boring a hole in the ear of a servant who chose to remain with his master rather than receive his freedom in the sabbatical year (Exod. 21:2-6). This speaks of a life of joy in service and obedience. According to the Septuagint and *Hebrews*, the metaphor is that of a body ready to do the will of God. Our hands and feet are to be given in God's service.

Hebrews regards Jesus, the word of God, as the one who speaks through all of the Scriptures, which are in another sense also the word of God. He is the one who can really live out the Scriptures. Therefore *Hebrews* presents these words from the Psalm as having been fulfilled in the life of Jesus (verse

5a). Tragically, people are prone to degeneration in every aspect of life – even in relationship with God. We tend to abuse and take for granted the gifts of God. This is what the Reformers were referring to when they spoke of our 'total depravity'. It was inevitable, then, that even within Israel most people would abuse the sacrificial system.

The key to a right relationship with God is a genuine desire to serve him, an attitude of obedience to him, and genuine repentance when we fail. Sacrifices were a stark reminder of the seriousness of sin, and a pledge of the cost of putting God first in our lives. They were never enough in themselves. Without the right attitude of love for God and repentance for sin, the sacrifices were simply an empty ritual. The prophets understood this perfectly, and constantly pleaded with the people to get the perspective right (e.g. 1 Sam. 15:22; Hos. 6:6; Mic. 6:6-8; Isa. 1:10-20). We also see this corrective teaching in the temple songbook itself (e.g. Pss. 50:14; 51:16-17).

Jesus is the only person to have obeyed God completely and purely. But he also made the perfect sacrifice – of himself. Again it must be emphasised that even although obedience and repentance were always the key issues, the sacrifices were also ordained by God, and were therefore also good. If there had been no value whatsoever in sacrifice, then Jesus would not have needed to have offered himself on the cross. He could simply have ignored the whole matter of sacrifice. The truth is, however, that sacrifice was a vital part of God's plan. Complete forgiveness and restoration of relationship with God requires both repentance and the shedding of blood (9:22).

Jesus came and lived the perfect life of obedience and purity. He was therefore able to offer the perfect sacrifice. Because of this, we are all able to have access to complete forgiveness, and the Holy Spirit can enable us to obey the Lord.

28. We should draw close to God and to one another (10:19-25)

The pastoral concern of *Hebrews* for his people becomes very evident at this point in the letter. Right to the end of the chapter we find *Hebrews* applying the teaching which he has been spelling out for these Jewish believers in Jesus. It is almost as if he is saying that Jesus has charged the batteries with an inexhaustible supply of potential energy, and that the responsibility of Jesus' followers is now to appropriate all of this blessing as dynamic energy. They are to **enter the Most Holy Place** and **draw near to God** (19-22), **hold unswervingly to the hope** (23-25), **remember those earlier days** (26-35), and **persevere** (36-39). It would break the heart of *Hebrews* if his people lost their vision and commitment.

But it is not only our commitment to God which *Hebrews* sees as vital to our spiritual and community health. We are to show the same love and commitment to one another as well. In verse 24 he encourages his readers to **consider how we may spur one another on**. This word 'consider' is the same verb which we found in 3:1, where it was translated 'fix your thoughts on'. It is a strong word which means to focus attention firmly on the matter at hand. *Hebrews* is saying here that we must truly endeavour to find ways to help one another to love and serve the Lord.

This concern to link service of God with service to one another reflects the teaching of Jesus himself. In response to a question as to the most important of all the commandments, Jesus responded by linking two commandments together:

> 'The most important one,' answered Jesus, 'is this: 'Hear, O Israel, the Lord our God, the Lord is one. Love the Lord your God with all your heart and with all your soul and with all your mind and with all your strength.' The second is this: 'Love your neighbour as yourself.' There is no commandment greater than these' (Mark 12:29-31).

There is a significant challenge to us all here. In what ways are we really trying to encourage other believers **towards love and good deeds**? Does my life make it easier for others to love and serve God? The call on each of us is to share the concern of *Hebrews* for the people of God.

It is worth noting here that whether or not *Hebrews* consciously intended to do so, we have a lovely echo in verses 22-24 of the inspirational trilogy of virtues. These three fundamental characteristics for believers of 'faith, hope and love' are most famously presented in 1 Corinthians 13:13. However they are found elsewhere too (e.g. 1 Thess. 1:3), and this section of *Hebrews* is one such passage. **Let us draw near to God with ... faith ... hold unswervingly to the hope ... spur one another on towards love ...** This is as godly as any encouragement could be!

A major aspect of our mutual encouragement is the regular **meeting together** of believers. *Hebrews* has already emphasised that we are all members of the same family, joint heirs and members of the same household (3:1, 6, 14), so it is obvious that we are obliged to care for one another. Our responsibility is not just to make sure of ourselves before God, as some seem to teach today.

Apparently some of the believers to whom *Hebrews* wrote were **in the habit** of staying away from such meetings. Such behaviour not only leaves the believer in an isolated and vulnerable relationship with the Lord, unable to receive the help and encouragement of the larger body, but it also deprives the other believers of that person's blessing and help. It is doubly dangerous and selfish.

The 'drawing near in faith' of verse 22 and the 'holding on to hope' of verse 23 might be possible in extraordinary circumstances of being done without the benefit of community life and worship. This happens with secret believers in various contexts.

But it is impossible to live out the exhortation of verse 24 unless we are involved in one another's lives and meeting one another regularly. Let us make sure that we are hearing this word from God clearly. What is more, this perspective would have been particularly valued in the Jewish community. Jewish people have always known the importance of regular worship and fellowship together, drawing strength and comfort from one another.

Many people have pointed out the similarity between the words here – **Let us not give up meeting together** – and the teaching of Hillel, one of Judaism's most respected leaders. Hillel lived at about the same time as Jesus, being an older contemporary. In a tractate of the Talmud devoted to ethical insights and principles, known as 'Chapters of the Fathers', one of Hillel's teachings is given: 'Hillel said: Do not set yourself apart from the community.' It is surprising to learn that some of the Jewish believers were going against the Jewish grain, let alone the will of the community of believers, by avoiding meetings.

Perhaps they were afraid of being too easily identified by opponents of the gospel if they were regularly seen to frequent the established meeting places? Were they afraid of persecution?

It is also striking that Hillel's words, quoted above, go on immediately to say: 'Do not be sure of yourself until the day of your death.' His point was that no one can assume that he can make it through life without the support and correction of the community. We are to be so aware of our own sinfulness and weakness that we know our need for others to help us to keep right with God. *Hebrews* also reflects this perspective. He encourages the believers to help one another **all the more as you see the Day approaching**. This is the day of judgment when we will give final account for our lives to God.

This serious issue of being accountable to God for our lives is developed in the next section of the letter. Jesus' return is not only a cause for rejoicing among believers as we wait for vindication and comfort, but it is also a reality which should help believers to resist temptation as we know we will face the Lord on that Day. Jesus told a parable making this very point in Luke 12:16-21. Paul was conscious of the need for this understanding, as is clear from passages such as 2 Corinthians 5:10. The perspective of coming judgment is brought out, as we shall see, in 10:27, 30-31; 12:14, 23-25.

Having said that, those who really follow Jesus in their lives can also have a real **confidence** that the death and resurrection of Jesus will enable them to **draw near to God**. This is not just for everyday life now, though that is certainly true, but also for entry into heaven itself, as it were. We can never afford to take this for granted, since that is also a proven way to presumption and spiritual and moral laxitude. It is not the triumphalistic cry of the person who sees him/herself as an impregnable castle, saying that he/she is perfectly safe from sin and weakness. It is rather the claim of the person who is modest about him/herself and yet is able to point to his/her relationship to Jesus and to say that confidence is in Jesus' love and sacrifice.

Jesus' death has **opened** up for us **a new and living way**. This is the theme of the whole letter. Our part is important too, of course. The gospel is not about magic. It involves a real relationship for it to be effective for us. Nor is it something which we have bought and can therefore do with as we like. We are the ones who have been bought with the price of Jesus' life. Therefore we can only have confidence if we have **a sincere heart**.

Our **hearts** must be **sprinkled to cleanse us** and our **bodies** must be **washed with pure water**. This is the language of the temple, reminding us that priests had to wash themselves thoroughly before they could enter the holy place (Lev. 16:4;

Exod. 29:4). It is possible that the phrase about having our
bodies washed is a reference to the need for baptism, but if
so, then the priority is still given to the need for clean hearts.
Without a clean heart baptism is ineffective (see 9:10). Many
today still treat baptism as if it were a kind of magic
performance and formula to guarantee salvation.

Hebrews will not allow this kind of thinking. The Day is
approaching, and we need to be ready to meet our God with
sincere and cleansed hearts.

29. We dare not take the gospel lightly (10:26-31)

This section of the letter should be treated very seriously.
Hebrews seems to have a group of people in mind – this is not
just a piece of hypothetical speculation. He is not simply
speaking about believers who have fallen into sin, a situation
which covers all of us from time to time. His focus is on those
who perhaps drifted away from the spiritual disciplines at one
point in their lives (2:1) and then began to drift away from
meeting regularly with the other believers (10:25). The
warning is to any who are in danger of actually turning their
backs on the Lord and the Lord's people.

Such people **deliberately keep on sinning** even though
they know **the truth** of God's means of salvation. To know
the right way and yet to walk away from it is a terrible
arrogance and insult to God. This is far more serious than the
sins of those who have never heard the gospel. The Jewish
believers to whom *Hebrews* was writing would have been
fully aware of the teaching of Amos 3:1-2 and its relevance
for this section of the letter:

> Hear this word the LORD has spoken against you, O people of Israel
> – against the whole family I brought up out of Egypt: 'You only
> have I chosen of all the families of the earth; therefore I will punish
> you for all your sins.'

The context of these verses in Amos shows that many peoples will be punished by God, but God's anger and disappointment are focused on Israel. She was the one who should have known better – not the Moabites, etc. Just so with believers in Jesus who turn their backs on him. *Hebrews* says here that it is as if such people have **trampled the Son of God under foot**. *Hebrews* reminds his readers that those whose sin was to have lived lives in which they **rejected the law of Moses** were guilty of sin punishable by death. How much more serious it is, he says, to have gone beyond breaking laws to breaking the heart of God!

Approaching it from another direction *Hebrews* says that such people have **treated as an unholy thing** the ultimate holy sacrifice – the death of Jesus for their sakes. To be holy in the teaching of the Hebrew Bible is to be 'set apart' from everyday use for the service of God. Therefore to treat Jesus' death as something 'unholy' is to regard it as merely something ordinary, something commonplace.

What is more, *Hebrews* goes on to say that such people have **insulted the Spirit of grace**. The Holy Spirit has come as a Guide and Teacher for the people of God (John 14:26; 16:13). He has come to convict us about sin in our lives (John 16:8). To walk away from the Lord is to insult the Holy Spirit.

The point is that by the time people have come to the stage of being able to reject the love of Jesus, having known that love in their lives, then they have gone beyond the context in which they can be saved. As he puts it, **no sacrifice for sins is left**. Jesus' death on the cross does not effect salvation for people against their will or when they have renounced their faith and rejected Jesus.

This is not about impersonal laws and sinful lives. It is about knowing, loving and serving the Lord – and then one day rejecting that relationship. We must pray that we will never come to such a point where we destroy our relationship with the Lord.

We must also pray that God will help us to help any believers we know who may be in danger of turning their backs on the Lord. However we must also make sure that we are not judgmental regarding others. It may be that the factor which led to the believers in that original congregation walking away from their faith was the awful persecution which they suffered. We shall look at this in the next section. The cost of discipleship can be high, and if we have not had to pay a high price then we had better not condemn others.

Love and prayer, expressed practically, are what is needed from the community of believers as we 'consider how we may spur one another on towards love and good deeds'. If we care for one another at all in the family of Jesus then we should be ready to intercede for and help anyone who might **fall into the hands of the living God**. That would be **a dreadful thing**, says *Hebrews*, and one which should make us all sober in preparation for the Day as it approaches.

30. We must stand fast in our faith (10:32-39)

Hebrews reminds his readers of **earlier days** when they had suffered **persecution** because of their faith in Jesus. He honours them as he says to them **you stood your ground**. It is possible that they stand in contrast with those in the previous section who decided that the cost was too high and walked away from Jesus. Believers who endure in this way receive our respect and can serve to inspire us to stand firm in our own situations.

Hebrews encourages them (and us) to keep our trust in God intact. We are not to **throw away** our **confidence** that it is worth the cost. To carry on for a moment with the metaphor of *paying a cost* for devotion to Jesus, and considering the cost to be worth it, *Hebrews* says that this confidence **will be richly rewarded**. Some of the believers had even **joyfully accepted the confiscation** of their property in this time of persecution because they knew that in Jesus they had **better and lasting possessions**. Those who **persevere** in the face of persecution will receive from God **what he has promised**.

In two contexts of speaking about persecution Jesus made this very point which *Hebrews* is now restating. In Matthew 10:22 when he is sending out his disciples to ministry 'like sheep among wolves', Jesus warns them that they will face hatred as a result of their devotion to him. But he then states that 'he who stands firm to the end will be saved.' In Matthew 24:13 as part of his sobering warnings about the signs of the end of this age, Jesus again speaks of hatred and persecution to come, and repeats his promise that 'he who stands firm to the end will be saved.'

Habakkuk 2:3-4 is quoted to re-enforce the need for trust in God through all difficult times. The term translated **shrink(s) back** comes from a root which means to take down and roll up a sail on a boat. The metaphor indicates people who lose hope and confidence in the course on which they are headed and so withdraw from the course. We must have sympathy with believers who lose confidence and hope and so change course, as it were. We should also try to understand those who withdraw from the course which leads to faith in Jesus because of a realisation of the cost which will be involved.

However, we are to do all that we can to help them to stand strong. God calls us to be strong in the Lord. Rather than shrinking back and being **destroyed**, we are to have faith, to **believe**, and be **saved**. There is a lovely and challenging play on words hidden here in the Hebrew language of faith. The Hebrew word for faith/trust comes from a root which means to be established, set, dependable. In other words, to trust in God is to know that he is absolutely established and that his word is completely dependable. To trust in God is also to be established in life.

This play on words is expressed beautifully in Isaiah 7:9 where the same Hebrew root is used twice, once in the sense of having faith and once in the sense of being established. Some translators have tried to convey something of this play on words in their translations:

> If you do not stand firm in your faith, you will not stand firm at all. (NIV)

> If your faith is not enduring, you will not endure. (GNB)

Having faith, then, is the opposite of shrinking back. To have faith in God is to spread the sails of our lives so that the Holy Spirit can blow us forward with God.

Attention must also be drawn in this section of the letter to the fact that those who did stand firm under persecution were also able to get alongside others who were suffering for their faith. *Hebrews* says to them, **you stood side by side with those who were so treated**. The word translated 'stood side by side with' comes from the same root (*koinonia*) that gives the term 'fellowship' in many translations. The verb means to share in partnership with someone.

It is used by Paul in two significant passages:

> just as you share in our sufferings, so also you share in our comfort (2 Cor. 1:7).

> I want to know the Messiah and the power of his resurrection and the fellowship of sharing in his sufferings (Phil. 3:10).

Peter also uses it in a context linking the experience of suffering for Jesus with the hope of glory:

> I appeal as a fellow-elder, a witness of the Messiah's sufferings and one who will also share in the glory to be revealed (1 Pet. 5:1).

This standing by those who are suffering for their faith is yet another honoured way to 'consider how we may spur one another on towards love and good deeds.' How important it is to stand by one another!

31. Faith is about trust in God (11:1-3)

Quite apart from this chapter *Hebrews* speaks about faith many times (4:2; 6:1-3, 12; 10:22, 39; 12:2; 13:7). In combination with its use in chapter 11, it becomes clear that the term 'faith' can refer not only to the content of what we believe but also, and perhaps more importantly, to the attitude or relationship of faith which describes and defines our walk with the Lord. Faith is not about intellectual belief with no room for doubt or questions, but rather about trusting God and being committed to following him whatever the circumstances.

This is not at all to say that doctrine is unimportant, but that the relationship with God is what counts at the end of the day. As James 2:19 says, even the demons know correct doctrine – but they don't live a life of faith. In chapter 11 we are about to be reminded of notable characters whose lives were characterised by this walk of faith with God. The fact that they all lived before the time of Jesus, and therefore did not have the full doctrinal truth of the gospel community, is of no significance in this context. There is nothing a believer in Jesus today could teach them about having faith in the Lord. Their faith is **what the ancients were commended for**.

In verse 1 we are told two things about faith. The word translated **sure of** has to do with the fundamental nature or structure of something, making it what it is. In one of its derived meanings it came to mean a 'title deed', and this is a helpful metaphor for us too. Faith is like a title deed to a property in that it acts as a guarantee that the unseen property, in this case the glory of eternal life with the Lord, really is ours.

Secondly, the word translated **certain of** was used to refer to the certainty in a judge's mind about a case or brief before him. In the same way, then, faith is like the confidence which comes from acting on a brief which cannot fail in court, but which has still to be actually worked out in the court.

It is a word about total trust, complete conviction and surrender to God's will and care. *Hebrews* takes us back to the basic context of our lives and says that it is faith that makes us sure that **the universe was formed at God's command**. This is God's world whatever others may say, or whatever may make us almost doubt it sometimes. The Nicene Creed has included this statement of faith within itself:

I believe in God the Father Almighty, Creator of heaven and earth, of all things, seen and unseen ...

What is more, *Hebrews* takes issue with the philosophical view which was current then that God actually created the world out of existing and flawed matter. This was understood to explain the suffering and imbalance in life. *Hebrews* declares that this is altogether God's world, and that it **was not made out of what was visible**. There was no inherent flaw in God's creation, rather the flaw came with mankind's rebellion and sin. We cannot know this in any 'scientific' way, but by faith we know it to be true.

Sometimes a life of faith will mean trusting God in a certain direction when the world is strongly advising us to move in another direction; sometimes it will mean trusting that God's purpose will be shown or the fulfilment of a promise will take place in the future in spite of an unpromising present.

Yet Jesus himself was concerned about finding faith in every generation. He told a parable about a widow who pestered a reluctant judge until he heard her case and gave her justice in order to get peace from her. Jesus taught that since God, unlike the judge, is good and committed to justice for his people, then his people should have real confidence that God will hear them and answer their prayers. But would the people have that confidence in God? Did they really have faith?

Jesus concluded the teaching with the haunting words:

However, when the Son of Man comes, will he find faith on the earth? (Luke 18:1-8)

Let us pray that we will be worthy of commendation for our faith, as the ancients were for theirs. We have the gift of the Messiah and the Holy Spirit to help us in a way that they did not have. And let us pray that our whole generation of believers will have real faith in the Lord.

32. The heroes and heroines of faith (A) (11:4-32)

We are now able to enjoy this parade of faithful men and women of God. But we will also need to be alert to the challenge which is being given by their lives.

Abel (verse 4)
In contrast to his brother, Cain, Abel brought **a better sacrifice**. In the Genesis account of this episode (Gen. 4:1-7) we are shown that Cain was not able to resist the power of temptation and eventually murdered his brother. Abel, we infer, was someone with a pure heart who offered his lamb in faith and love of God. Jesus testifies to Abel's true heart (Matt. 23:35), and John bears witness to Cain's evil nature (1 John 3:12).

Abel was willing to offer his best to the Lord trusting that he would have a purpose for this. We can learn this lesson from him for ourselves, trusting it to be true, since it is a part of our Scripture.

Enoch (verses 5-6)

Enoch's story is told in Genesis 5:18, 21-24, and this mysterious figure features in the Scripture alongside Elijah as someone who did not die a natural death. At least it is not stated that he died. Elijah was taken up in a chariot at the end of his life (2 Kgs. 2:1-12), but of Enoch it is simply stated that he 'walked with God; then he was no more, because God took him away'.

This might be taken to mean that he died when it says that he 'was no more'. Jewish traditions have it, however, that he was somehow transported to heaven without tasting death. *Hebrews* says the same when it tells us that **he did not experience death**. It was because of his life of faith that God gave him this gift of transportation to heaven.

We are told that **he was commended as one who pleased God**. We have had to mention the Septuagint before in this commentary: the Greek translation of the Hebrew Bible completed in the middle of the third century before Jesus' birth. The Septuagint actually has a different text in Genesis 5:24 from the Hebrew. Instead of saying that Enoch 'walked with God', as in the Hebrew, the Greek has it that Enoch 'was well pleasing to God'. Perhaps this version was in *Hebrews*' mind as he wrote this chapter?

At any rate *Hebrews* knows that there is an important teaching about faith to be made in this regard. Without living a life of faith **it is impossible to please God**. In fact we are told in Genesis 5:21-22 that it was only when he was 65 years old that Enoch walked with God. Perhaps, in the light of *Hebrews*, we can speculate that he only came to a life of faith at that time in his life (connected with the responsibilities of parenthood?) and that his change of life was what pleased God? It is never too late to trust in God.

The final part of this portion on Enoch can seem anticlimactical. James says that belief in the existence of God is not enough (Jas. 2:19), and hope for a reward may strike us as compromising service for the sake of God alone. Yet it is written here that to come to God in faith people must believe that **he exists** and that **he rewards**. God is generous to **those who earnestly seek him**. Are we being told here that Enoch was alone in his generation in his faith in the true God and that God would look after those who sought to live their lives in accordance with his will?

Noah (verse 7)

Noah, like Enoch before him, 'walked with God' (Gen. 6:9). His story is found in Genesis 5:28-9:29, associated especially with the account of the flood which God sent to punish that wicked generation of mankind. Noah stood out in that generation as the one who listened when he was **warned**, trusted about **things not yet seen**, acted **in holy fear**, and **built an ark** in spite of ridicule. In other words, he was a man of real faith.

Because of his faith he was able to **save his family**; he was able to put the world to shame as it became clear that only he had a relationship of faith with God, which is what is meant by saying that he **condemned the world**; and he **became heir of the righteousness that comes by faith**. The first result speaks for itself, but the second and third deserve a comment.

Noah did not condemn those who died in the flood. God was responsible for the flood and its effects. Nor did Noah forbid others from building arks if they had chosen to follow his example. In that sense they condemned themselves by not listening to God or Noah. Noah's witness to God condemned everyone else in the sense that they did not heed his life and trust in God. Our witness to the Lord can be a powerful testimony in our generation, too, at least in our own circles of friends and colleagues.

With regard to becoming an heir of the righteousness which

is only available to those who live a life of faith, this is a
fundamental point which Paul knew was needed by the
community of believers in Rome (see Rom. 1:17; 3:22; 4:13;
9:30). God justifies us when he knows that we really put our
trust in him for salvation and righteousness. Noah would have
been a lonely man of faith in his generation, but he was the
one whom God declared righteous (Gen. 7:1).

Abraham (verses 8-19)
Abraham has already featured in *Hebrews* 6:13-15 as the
person who received a promise from God, which he saw
realised in his life as a result of his patience and faith. Abraham
is the father of the Jewish people in Jewish tradition, the
archetypal figure of faith, and this view of him as their ancestor
in the faith is reflected in *Hebrews* 2:16. Paul also knows the
importance of Abraham as the father of the faithful servants
of God (Rom. 4; Gal. 3). Already in the days of Israel's exile
in Babylon Abraham was held up as a model of faith (Neh.
9:7-8). What do we learn about the life of faith from this man?

Verses 8-10
When he was **called** by God to trust him and go to a new life
in a new place, he **obeyed and went**. At that point the
inheritance was all in the future (see Gen. 12:1-4). His
obedience, like that of Noah and others, stemmed from his
complete trust in God and his confidence that God would keep
his promises. He could not **know where he was going**, but he
did trust that God knew best and would not let him down.
Abraham was willing to leave behind everything familiar,
reassuring and supportive in order to follow God into an
unknown future, and this willingness and courage to sacrifice
for God was a characteristic which is presented to us as
something to try to imitate in our own lives.

Abraham lived in faith his whole life, **like a stranger in a**

foreign country. There were already people living **in the promised land**, and these residents lived in towns and cities. Abraham, his children and his grandchildren lived in tents. It was to be some generations before the children of Israel settled in and built urban centres for life in the country. If building cities symbolises a sense of real belonging and the putting down of roots, to change the metaphor, then the fact that Abraham and his family **lived in tents** symbolises that they were still waiting for the time of inheritance.

Hebrews tells us that Abraham was able to live like this because he was not fixed on materialistic goals, and nor did he demand that God act on Abraham's terms. He was focused on another city altogether, **the city with foundations, whose architect and builder is God**. For the person of faith it is preferable to live in a tent waiting for God to provide what he has promised than to build one's own city. To use the same mixed metaphor as above, God's foundations for our lives are better than any roots we may try to put down.

Verses 11-12

A second aspect of the promise which was given to Abraham when he was called by God into a covenant relationship was that he would be the father of a huge family of descendants, **as numerous as the stars in the sky**. By the time that the covenant heir, Isaac, was born, Sarah was well past the age for being able to conceive and Abraham was also **past age**. Humanly speaking, this couple could not have their own child. Yet God had said that they would. Hagar's son, Ishmael, was not the one, since he was only the child of Abraham.

Only extraordinary faith could have trusted God for a son at that stage in their lives, and Abraham had that faith. And yet he had not always had it, as if it were some sort of automatic response. Faith is forged in the furnace of life, and both Abraham and Sarah had laughed when they first heard God say that they would have a son at their advanced years (Gen. 17:17; 18:12). But Abraham came to appreciate the power of God. Not only that, but he came to know that God **who had made the promise** is **faithful**.

Faithful as applied to God means that he is true to himself and keeps his word and his promises. You can absolutely depend on God. Faithful as applied to people like Abraham means that they do depend on God and trust him absolutely. Abraham's body may have been **as good as dead**, but his faith was alive and strong.

Verses 13-16
Hebrews inserts here a comment on the characteristics of Abraham and his family in their walk with God. They were all **living by faith when they died**, meaning that although the promises of God were like their life-blood they never knew the joy of experiencing the fulfilment of those promises. They **saw** the fulfilment with the certainty of visionaries, and were so confident that the promises would be realised that, to use *Hebrews'* lovely phrase, they **welcomed them from a distance**.

Perhaps we have here an echo of the experience of Moses who himself never came into the inheritance of the promised land? He only saw it from a distance, as we read in Deuteronomy 3:23-28. The situation is quite different, of course. Moses was told that Joshua would lead the people into the land as a result of Moses being disciplined by God for his *lack of faith* in the incident of the miracle of finding water in the wilderness (Num. 20:1-13).

Can we imagine how profoundly disappointed and frustrated Moses must have been to be so near and yet so far? Yet he could 'know' that entry into the promised land was very close. Abraham was under no discipline for lack of faith – rather he was commended for his faith. He could have no idea what was to transpire between his death and the entry into the promised land under Joshua's leadership.

The **distance** as far as Moses was concerned was essentially one of geographical space as he looked down from Mount Pisgah to see the last few miles to be covered. Abraham was looking at a distance of generations, and he really needed the eyes of faith. His immediate descendants were no different in this.

Hebrews goes on to say that they **admitted** that they were **aliens and strangers on earth**. What does it mean that they 'admitted' this? Surely not that they were, as it were, 'interrogated' by others in Canaan until they confessed to being a community of faith looking to God for their identity and destiny? It is likely that this means that they not only knew among themselves what their lives were, but shared their conviction with others. Whether they took the initiative in this, or responded to the natural questions which the Canaanites would ask of these newcomers, it speaks of a willingness to bear witness to God and to his call upon their lives.

They testified to others that they were **aliens and strangers**. Could this be a badge of honour? It sounds like a social category which people would rather keep quiet about! We certainly know that the patriarchs were semi-nomadic, wandering in the region in which they lived (Gen. 12:6-10; 13:1-12, 17-18; 14:13-16; 20:1; 21:34; 22:19; 23:4; 26:3-4; 35:12,27). In actual fact *Hebrews* uses three different words to describe the transient nature of the patriarchal way of life – how might they apply to believers today?

The first word was used in 11:9 where Abraham was described as being like 'a stranger' in a foreign country. This term is used of people who are given permission, as it were, to live in a country or region. Such people were just above slaves in the social strata, and often had to pay taxes in return for permission to settle. They were always labelled as outsiders and never accepted by the host community. They were almost like tenants in the host country. Abraham, as a man of faith, did not belong in the world, but was only living here temporarily.

In the section which we are looking at, in 11:13, two other words are used. **Aliens** translates a word which refers to strangers or foreigners with overtones of contempt and fear. It gives us the word xenophobia in English, meaning fear of or hatred of foreigners. Such people are actually rejected by those who regard them as aliens. So perhaps *Hebrews* is hinting here at the opposition which there was to the people of Israel as they moved towards and then settled in the promised land?

The third term used, translated by **strangers**, is simply a term for people who have made a permanent home in one place but who are temporarily living somewhere else. This describes the patriarchal families and all believers very well.

The point which is stressed by the use of these terms is that God's people do not belong, and should not see themselves as belonging, to this world and its goals and ways. We are pilgrims on our way through this part of our lives to the **better country** which lies before us – home with the Lord in eternity. Abraham knew this and taught his family well.

One of the dangers or drawbacks of having a movement started by a charismatic figure is that when he/she dies, or when his/her successor dies, it can be hard for the followers to maintain the vision and drive. If only the founder has 'heard' the Lord or 'seen' the vision, then those who follow need to depend on second-hand revelation. In difficult times this is often not enough and the movement will fragment or fade away. We shall see the particular relevance of this when we explore the faith by which Abraham was willing to sacrifice his son, Isaac.

This could have happened with the death of father

Abraham. The first or second generation of his descendants might have felt too vulnerable living on the strength of his relationship with God and decided to return 'home' to the region of Ur. They certainly **would have had opportunity to return**. But the faith lived on, and they knew that their future was with God. They were **longing for a better country – a heavenly one**. Ultimately, *Hebrews* is teaching us, home for the people of God can only be where God himself is.

This perspective is found elsewhere in the New Testament as well. Both Paul and Peter encourage their readers to think along these lines:

> our citizenship is in heaven (Phil. 3:20).

> live your lives as strangers here in reverent fear (1 Pet. 1:17).

> Dear friends, I urge you, as aliens and strangers in the world, to abstain from sinful desires, which war against your soul (1 Pet. 2:11).

Because **these people** exhibited this perspective in their lives, then in spite of the fact that we know that they still made serious mistakes in their lives, a fact which Scripture makes sure we know, they were still God's people, looking to him and to his promises. Therefore God was **not ashamed to be called their God**. This does not mean that we can live our lives as we choose and presume upon God to stick by us, but it does mean that God is faithful to his covenant promises and that he can forgive us for our sins if our hearts are really set on loving and serving him.

Genuine repentance and commitment to live a faithful and holy life are necessary, but with God it is his love and commitment which are the key factors.

Verses 17-19

This section takes us back to Genesis 22:1-14 and the unbelievable test of Abraham's trust in God when God asked

him to sacrifice the heir of the covenant promises (Gen. 21:12).
What could be in God's mind to kill the very one who was to
carry on the community of faith? Yet Abraham, **when God
tested him**, obeyed and all but **offered Isaac as a sacrifice**
when the Lord stepped in at the last moment and stopped him.

As far as Abraham was concerned, of course, Isaac was
going to die on that place of sacrifice, and *Hebrews* tells us
that humanly speaking he would have had to believe that God
would raise Isaac from the dead in order to use him as the one
to continue the covenant community. He was as good as dead
in Abraham's mind at the point when the Lord stepped in to
prevent the death, and so Abraham did **receive Isaac back
from death, figuratively speaking**. Abraham's great faith
was justified.

In the next verse Isaac is mentioned as another hero of
faith, but interestingly it is not in connection with this incident
of his near sacrifice. I think that we should pause for a moment
to reflect on the faith which Isaac must have had to have trusted
his father at that tense time. Many believers suppose, without
thinking about it, that Isaac must have been a mere toddler
when he went with Abraham to Mount Moriah. However, if
you read the narratives in Genesis it is clear that Isaac must
have been a mature man by that stage.

Therefore Abraham could hardly have overpowered his
son and forced him to lie down as a sacrifice to the Lord. He
might have knocked him out and bound him, it is true, but
that is hardly the picture presented in Scripture! Isaac must
have had faith too, and perhaps more than his father, since he
was the one about to die. Not only that, but since it was
Abraham who heard the word from God about this, and not
Isaac, it meant that Isaac was also showing great faith in his
father and in Abraham's relationship with God.

When we ask ourselves in this context whether we have
Abraham's faith, we might do well to ask whether we also
have Isaac's faith.

Isaac (verse 20)

This blessing is to be found in Genesis 27:28-29, 39-40. Isaac is close to death as he gives his blessing (Gen. 27:2). Isaac died a wanderer in the region, not yet seeing the fulfilment of the promise given to his father. Nevertheless he died in hope, passing on the blessing to the next generation to nurture and trust.

There is a difficulty in the text, however. Isaac believed that he was giving his blessing to Esau, the first born. With the aid of Jacob's mother Jacob deceived his father and so received the blessing. In one sense, then, Isaac acted out of weakness, but his faith in the future with God was strong nevertheless. God was able to bless and use someone as deceptive and ambitious as Jacob, and this is also an act of grace which should comfort all believers. It is not a licence to live as we like, but simply a reassurance that God can use very ordinary, weak and sinful people for his purposes.

As a matter of interest, Esau's rising against and over Jacob, as expressed in Isaac's blessing on Esau, can be said to have taken place when King Herod ruled in the land of Israel. Herod was an Idumean, which is to say an Edomite, and they were descendants of Esau.

Jacob (verse 21)

The account of Jacob's blessing is given in Genesis 48:9-20. Note how the second born was given priority over the first born, just as in Jacob's own generation. Once again the sovereign grace and choice of God is seen to be in control of history, not the rules of primogeniture or any other rules, no matter how useful in ordinary circumstances. Note also that Jacob was close to death (Gen. 47:29).

We note that both Isaac and Jacob are said to have been weak as well as old at the time of giving their blessings. Both had very poor eyesight (Gen. 27:1; 48:10) and Jacob had to

lean on a support (whether his staff or the head of his bed) to
stand before God (Gen. 47:31). But for both, their faith in the
future with God was as strong as their bodies were weak. Jacob
too died in hope rather than fulfilment.

Joseph (verse 22)

Joseph is the third of the descendants of Abraham who is cited
by *Hebrews*. The incident is recorded in Genesis 50:22-26.
Here again we have a man close to death (Gen. 50:24) who
declares his faith in God's promises for a glorious future in
spite of the restricted circumstances of the present. He knew
that somehow God would have to deliver them from the hold
of the Egyptians and return them to the promised land. He did
not know what God would do, but he had faith for what later
generations were to call **the exodus**.

What is more, he was so confident of this that he left
instructions that his bones were to be taken with the returning
people to be buried in the land promised by God. This was
duly carried out centuries later (Exod. 13:19; Josh. 24:32).
This must have given a great deal of inspiration to Joseph's
people to see the faith of Joseph. We should never under-
estimate the value of showing faith for the whole community
of believers. Our own faith can grow in a community of faith,
and this is surely an important reason for not giving up
'meeting together' (10:25).

Moses' parents (verse 23)

The story of their action is to be found in Exodus 2:1-10. The
king had decreed that all baby boys born in the community of
the Hebrew slaves should be killed at birth so as to control
that community (Exod. 1:15-22). Moses, second in importance
only to Abraham in Israel's story before the coming of Jesus,
would not even have been born without the faith of his parents.
They could see that he was **no ordinary child**. In spite of the
king's decree **they were not afraid**.

After hiding Moses for three months, they arranged for him to be 'found' by the king's daughter and brought up in safety at the palace. God honoured their faith and Moses was raised safely, with his own mother as his nursing mother at the royal court (Exod. 2:1-10).

Moses' parents' faith in the face of the community's fear is emphasised here, and we can probably assume that *Hebrews* has done this deliberately. We have had cause on a few occasions to mention the fear of the Jewish believers to whom this letter was written, and it is likely that he was aware of the fear of persecution in some families to whom he wrote. The Roman Empire, as that of Egypt many centuries before, was a cruel one, and royal decrees against believers were likely to come with increasing frequency. Therefore the inspiring example of these parents of Moses would strike a chord for the readers.

Moses (verses 24-28)
Having been brought up in the faith of his parents, Moses went on to show his own lack of fear of the royal court by spending time with his own people, the oppressed Hebrew slaves (Exod. 2:11-14). One day he saw one of his people, **the people of God**, being beaten by an Egyptian guard, and in a mixture of solidarity with his people and inappropriate aggression he killed the guard. We have to assume that he had heard about his real origins and the nature of the faith community from his mother, and that this had challenged him to somehow establish contact with his people.

Because of his identification with the community he intervened on their behalf in the killing of the guard who had personified the oppressive regime of Egypt against God's people. When he realised that this killing had been witnessed, albeit by one of the slaves, he could have arranged for the silencing of the witness, using his influence at court and trusting that a Hebrew slave would receive no justice. But, as

Hebrews says, he refused to be known as the son of Pharaoh's daughter. He did not try to silence his fellow Hebrew. As a result, the Pharaoh heard about the incident from others and Moses was no longer honoured or protected at court. He fled to Midian (Exod. 2:15).

This whole scenario came about because Moses did not forsake his faith for **the pleasures of sin** or **the treasures of Egypt**. *Hebrews* says that he put higher value on **disgrace for the sake of the Messiah**. So he committed himself to his true people and having met with the Lord in the wilderness he prepared to leave Egypt. This he did **by faith, not fearing the king's anger** as the king pursued the slaves with his chariot forces to bring them back. He was **looking ahead** to the future with God. The verb in this case is one which means to fix one's eyes on something. Moses was completely focused on God's way so that other possibilities faded into the background.

Moses **persevered** in all this because throughout **he saw him who is invisible**. Moses had a particularly close relationship with the Lord and this is what kept his faith alive and his courage high. In one place we read that whereas God revealed himself to others by way of visions and dreams, he spoke to Moses 'mouth to mouth' (Num. 12:6-8). A similar phrase is used in Deuteronomy 34:10 where we are told that God knew Moses 'face to face'. The privilege of knowing the Lord personally is there for all believers in Jesus, and this should strengthen our faith and resolve to follow the Lord in all circumstances.

The recipients of this letter are being encouraged to share the conviction of Moses that suffering disgrace and worse for the sake of the Messiah is preferable to the life of relative ease and security which compromise with the world brings.

Moses **kept the Passover**, both before they left Egypt, associated with the last of the ten plagues, involving **the**

sprinkling of blood on the lintels of their houses to spare them from the visit of the angel of death, and thereafter in commemoration of the Exodus (Exod. 12:12-50). Is *Hebrews* again saying something to the Jewish believers to whom he is writing? If they were fearful of the threat of death and persecution because of their faith in Jesus then was *Hebrews* inspiring them to have the same faith as Moses? The blood of Jesus shed on the cross is far more effective than the blood of the lambs sprinkled on the lintels of people's houses.

We need to take note of the fact that in verse 26 *Hebrews* says that Moses endured all this **for the sake of the Messiah**. Moses did not know Jesus, nor could he have known the full picture of who the Messiah would be and how he would fulfil his role. So in what sense did he suffer for the Messiah? It would seem that *Hebrews* is telescoping the Messianic promises and the coming of Jesus, the Messiah, in this verse. In the sense that Moses was needed to keep alive the promises of God and to restore the community of God to the promised land, he was preparing the way for the coming Messiah.

Hebrews is saying to his people that they should try to be more like Moses in their faith, even to the extent of being prepared to suffer for Jesus' sake, and all the more so because, unlike Moses, they do know the Messiah. This is surely true for us as well!

Moses' generation (verse 29)

In Exodus 14 we read the story of the actual crossing of the Sea of Reeds (the so-called **Red Sea**). The miracle of the crossing is well enough known, but we need to remind ourselves that at first it was only Moses who had any faith for the crossing of the Sea. When the people were standing on the edge of the Sea with the Egyptian army closing fast they were 'terrified' and panicked (Exod. 14:10-12). Moses gave the words of encouragement which changed their hearts.

He told the people that the Lord himself would fight for them, so that they only needed to trust him and wait for the way to open before them (Exod. 14:13-14). At that point he was told to simply stretch his staff over the water to divide it. Moses and the people obeyed and trusted the Lord and he worked the miracle of redemption.

Once again we see *Hebrews* telling his people to trust God as the Israelites did. The terrible trials before them were serious, but no more difficult for God than the Sea and the Egyptian army which had had the people of God caught in a pincer trap all those generations ago. If these Jewish believers were frightened then that was all right in the sense that Moses' generation had started out that way too. What they had to do now was take Moses' words to heart:

The LORD will fight for you; you need only to be still (Exod. 14:14).

[Joshua] (verse 30)

Joshua is written in parentheses here simply because he is not mentioned in the text, although it is clear from the context that he is the hero of faith who is being considered. The story of the fall of Jericho is found in Joshua 6:1-20. It was a particularly significant fortified city which stood in Israel's way as she came in to settle in the promised land, and it took a miracle to see it fall to the people of Israel.

In fact it took faith as strong as Noah's to capture Jericho. Noah was told by God to build an ark far from the sea in the trust that the deluge would come, a building project which would have been ridiculed by his contemporaries. Joshua and the people of Israel were told by God not to fight to capture the city but to march around it for seven days with the ark of the covenant in front of them, symbolising the Lord's presence and leadership, and with the priests blowing trumpets. This too would have been hard for some Israelites to take seriously at first, and the people of Jericho would have ridiculed it mercilessly. It took real faith for Joshua to lead the Israelites in this plan to take the city.

One major point which *Hebrews* was making to his readers was that even in their increasingly difficult situation God was well able to protect them and win battles for them miraculously. The world's weapons are not the weapons which God uses in spiritual warfare. Alongside this was perhaps the point that just as Joshua and his people had to wait for seven days to see Jericho fall, so too the believers would need to have a faith which would be patient, waiting for God to act in his own time as well as in his own way. A lesson we still need to learn.

Rahab (verse 31)

Here we have the significant example of one person in Jericho who did *not* ridicule the people of Israel as they marched around the city. Rahab's story is told in Joshua 2:1-21, with the climax coming in 6:25, after the city has been taken. It would have meant death for her had she been found out to have protected and helped two of the Israelites. Rahab was a prostitute, and we are surprised to find someone with such an immoral profession and lifestyle being singled out as a heroine of faith. Yet James also singles her out as worthy of honour as a result of her courageous hiding of the scouts sent out by Joshua (Jas. 2:25).

Not only that, but she is even listed in Matthew's genealogy of Jesus himself (Matt. 1:5). She may not have been a model of righteous living, but even she was able to see that the Lord was with Israel and that his purposes would not be thwarted (Josh. 2:8-12). This certainty, or faith, that God would bring victory to the Israelites was exemplary, coming from someone who was not one of the covenant community. Her faith contrasts with the lack of faith shown by the scouts (with the exceptions of Caleb and Joshua) who were sent by Moses to spy out the land and the cities (Num. 13). And so the Lord is not ashamed to have her name appear in the list of his human ancestors.

We must be open to finding faith in the most unexpected people. Of course God demands that our lifestyles change when we belong to him, but redemption comes before sanctification! Let us never be judgmental about people.

Judges (verse 32)

Hebrews now collapses a number of heroes into one verse – was he running out of space on his writing material? He mentions three of the 'judges' who ruled over Israel in days where it was lamented that the tendency was for people to do what they wanted with their own lives (Judg. 6:10; 17:6). The lack of faith and the backsliding are highlighted by the fact that people then who had any faith in God, people like Gideon, looked back to the 'golden age' when God was active in Israel's life and lamented the perception that God had abandoned them (Judg. 6:13).

Gideon was such a man of God whose faith was under pressure as he looked around and saw that the Lord had seemed to have turned away from Israel. He was frightened and all too aware of his own weakness (Judg. 6:15). Yet he showed true faith by trusting God when the moment came, and thereby defeated the Midianites with only 300 men, underlining the fact that this was a miraculous intervention by God once more (Judg. 7).

Here is a lesson of faith: to be ready when the moment comes to actually trust in the Lord and move forward with him whatever the situation. The Jewish believers then and we now need to hear this.

The story of **Samson** is told in Judges 13-16. He was guilty of remarkable naïveté regarding the ways of the world and some arrogance concerning the gift of strength and fighting ability which the Lord had given him (Judg. 16), and so he was not an ideal person either. His eyes were not always on the Lord, and it was only when the Lord allowed the Philistines to take away his sight that he really came to see the realities of life and committed himself sacrificially to God and his service (Judg. 16:21-30).

We learn here that even people whose lives are compromised may yet have their finest hour before them if they hear the Lord and commit themselves to him at a crucial point.

Jephthah is best known for his vow to the Lord that if the Lord gave victory over the Ammonites then he would offer as a burnt offering the first animal that he saw coming out of his house when he returned from the battle (Judg. 11:30-31). He was anticipating that an animal would be seen coming out from a distance, but of course it was his only child, his daughter, and she was duly offered to the Lord (Judg. 11:34-39).

Jephthah had begun life as the child of a prostitute, and his family had driven him away to an outlaw life of some sort (Judg. 11:1-3). When relations with the Ammonites deteriorated to a situation of war the leaders of Israel called on Jephthah to return to be their leader, and he dealt with Israel's enemies in a very statesman-like manner before trusting God for victory (Judg. 11:12-27). He knew that though he might be termed a 'judge' over Israel, it was the Lord who had to be trusted for victory and leadership:

Let the LORD, the Judge, decide the dispute this day ... (Judg. 11:27).

Again we see an unlikely leader of God's people, but his simple faith was the factor which made him useful to the Lord. The lesson is there again for us. The judges were people whose faith and lives were less than perfect, and they inspire us to believe that we can also therefore be useful to God with our own less than perfect faith and lives.

Barak (verse 32)

General Barak was another whose faith at first was very fragile, and he needed the security of the support of Deborah, the prophetess and judge of Israel, before stepping out in faith (Judg. 4:8). Under God an amazing victory was won by Barak and his forces. He knew that the honour for victory would therefore be given to a woman (Judg. 4:9), a state of affairs which in that culture would have been considered shameful by most men, and yet he was prepared to be in the second rank of heroes and heroines as long as God's will was done.

This example of trust and humility is also a good lesson for all people of faith to learn.

King David (verse 32)

David is another hero of faith whose life was far short of perfect (e.g. 2 Sam. 11:2-27). He had been chosen by God, much to everyone's surprise, as the anointed king over Israel in succession to Saul (1 Sam. 16:1-13). It is one of the main teachings of this chapter in *Hebrews* that God may often surprise us by his choices and people may often surprise us with the faith they show under difficult circumstances.

David's faith, in spite of lapses in his character, is also shown in many ways, for example his complete trust that God was with him when he went out to fight for God's honour against Goliath with only his slingshot as a weapon (1 Sam. 17:1-54). He was a man after God's heart and was chosen as the ancestor of the Messiah himself, showing the Lord's commitment to a dynasty which would have more than its share of corrupt and faithless kings.

Faith often involves looking above the disappointing realities of life as we see it in order to focus on the Lord and his faithfulness.

Samuel and the prophets (verse 32)

Perhaps surprising to Christians today, *Hebrews* chooses Samuel, rather than Amos or Isaiah, etc., as the representative of the prophets. Whereas most Christians would probably cite one of the three major writing prophets as the key prophet, in Jewish tradition the greatest of the prophets is definitely held to be Moses (Deut. 34:10). However in other contexts where Moses is celebrated as the mediator of the Torah, Jewish tradition also cites Elijah as the most appropriate prophetic representative.

Looked at from a third perspective, a significant difference in the ways that Jewish Bibles and Christian Old Testaments are organised lies in the definition of prophetic books. In Christian tradition these books are the three major books of Isaiah, Jeremiah and Ezekiel, and the so-called minor prophets – including Daniel. In Jewish tradition Daniel is not held to be a prophetic book and, more importantly for us in the present context, the books of Joshua, Judges, Samuel and Kings are seen as vital prophetic books. Therefore Samuel can clearly be seen as an important early prophet, paving the way for those who follow.

Samuel suits *Hebrews* nicely, since he was a judge/prophet, therefore linking with the judges in the verse, and since he was the prophet who anointed David as king over Israel, therefore linking with David in this same compact verse. Samuel lived in extremely difficult times for the people of God and ploughed a lonely furrow for much of the time. In fact this was true for all of the prophets in some way or another.

Believers who are called into a prophetic ministry or into other positions of leadership within the community need to be prepared to walk a lonely path from time to time in the same way. What is often referred to as a 'prophetic distance' is necessary if leaders are to serve God without being submerged by the fears and desires of the people whom they

are called to serve. But this is also sometimes part of the call
of God on his people generally – to be willing to serve him at
the cost of popularity and constant affirmation.

Yet Samuel's sons did not keep the faith alive in their turn
and brought shame to his name (1 Sam. 8:1-5). This situation
has been seen in probably every generation of believers. Was
Samuel somehow at fault in this? Leaders in the Christian
community often neglect their own families in their zeal for
the Lord's work, and it is not rare to find their children turning
their backs on the option of Christian service for themselves.
The point here is that even Samuel had a mark of shame in his
family life and yet was undoubtedly a man of great faith.

33. The heroes and heroines of faith (B) (11:33-40)

In these verses *Hebrews* summarises the kind of victories
which people of faith have experienced under God's
leadership. Those who **conquered kingdoms** will include
people like Joshua and David, mentioned in this chapter. Those
who **administered justice** would bring to mind David again,
but also the judges given in this list of heroes and heroines.
Daniel is obviously the one in mind as the person for whom
the angel **shut the mouths of lions** (Dan. 6:21-23). Perhaps
Daniel and his friends in Babylon were also in mind as those
for whom God **quenched the fury of the flames** (Dan. 3: 23-
25). A number of people in the Hebrew Bible would fit the
bill as people who **escaped the edge of the sword**...

Hebrews says that **women received back their dead**, and
our minds go to the widow of Zarephath and the Shunammite
woman (1 Kgs. 17:8-24; 2 Kgs. 4:8-37). Their faith was strong
enough to believe that God could raise their sons from death.
Jesus himself spoke about prophets who were 'persecuted'
(Matt. 5:11-12), and perhaps this includes the various
descriptions of being **tortured**, facing **jeers and flogging**,
being **chained and put in prison**, being **stoned** and being

put to death by the sword (see also, for example, Jer. 20: 37-38; 2 Chr. 24:20-21; 1 Kgs. 22:24; 2 Kgs. 6:31-32).

Those who **wandered in deserts and mountains**, etc. would include people like Elijah and Elisha (1 Kgs. 18–19; 2 Kgs. 2:14). It is not just referring to times of persecution when such men of faith might flee to live in the wilderness, but also describes a chosen way of life by people who did not feel comfortable in the compromised royal courts and cities. They felt closer to God in the desert and mountainous regions, and were more able to practise a pure lifestyle there.

Sheepskins and goatskins would have been a preferred clothing as well as perhaps reflecting poverty and alienation from 'society' in some cases. John the Baptist chose such a lifestyle as we see in Matthew 3:4. *Hebrews* says rather poignantly and profoundly of these people that **the world was not worthy of them**. If only the world had faith in God and was following him then they would see the real value of a simple life trusting God for everything.

Hebrews also refers to some people of faith being **sawn in two** for their stand for the Lord, yet there is no biblical passage which corroborates this. What we do know is that there is a Jewish apocryphal book called 'The Ascension of Isaiah', and in 5:11-14 we read there the tradition that Isaiah indeed was killed by being sawn in two. It is likely that *Hebrews* and his Jewish readers would have been familiar with that tradition (which may of course be true, for all that it is a tradition rather than something recorded in Scripture).

Why would *Hebrews* include it here? His examples are all intended to inspire courage and faith in his readers. Here are role models to emulate, people who knew about real faith in the context of persecution and despair, and therefore worthy role models for his frightened and weak flock. What they did not need to hear were stories of faith in easy contexts. Jesus himself suffered for his ministry on our behalf (see, for example, Matt. 27:27-31, 32-50), so why should his followers expect to escape from all unpleasantness and difficulty in life?

Should we be listening carefully to this message in our day when there are so many who are preaching a triumphalistic message which tries to ignore or sublimate the hard realities of a faithful life for so many believers?

In the last two verses of the chapter *Hebrews* underlines a highly significant fact for his readers. Everyone mentioned and referred to in the chapter died having proven themselves worthy of being **commended for their faith**, and yet none of them saw the coming of the Messiah. None of them **received what had been promised** – to live in the Messianic Age. We who live after the birth of Jesus are heirs to a long tradition of faith and in a way those who went before us are only completed or **made perfect** in community with us.

We have the incomparable blessing of knowing Jesus, the Messiah, and we dare not take it for granted or treat it casually. They are all the more challenging as people of faith when we realise the huge advantage we have over them and yet how much we could still learn from them. **God had planned something better for us**, it says. How can we shrink from the challenge of being part of this inheritance of faith for those coming after us? That was the message given by *Hebrews* to his own struggling congregation.

34. The positive value of God's discipline (12:1-13)

In chapter 12 *Hebrews* picks up exactly from where he left off. The opening words are among the most famous in literature, expressing beautifully the teaching which we refer to in some Christian traditions as 'the communion of saints'. We are **surrounded** by **a great cloud of witnesses** who have gone before us in the faith, and we belong together as the family of God. It is a tremendous source of comfort and inspiration to realise that we are part of a family which not only numbers millions of believers across the world today, but also includes many millions of believers who have since died and gone to be with the Lord!

Hebrews says that this should help us to live lives of faith in our own generation and situation, not only because we know we are not alone even if at times we are tempted to feel that we are, but also because so many of the witnesses before us lived in equally or more difficult circumstances and maintained their faith and passed it on to the next generation.

In the same way, *Hebrews* goes on to say that we need look no further than Jesus himself. The Messiah endured the worst suffering of all and came through it to enable us to follow him. We are to **consider** Jesus who **endured such opposition** in his life for us, so that we might be inspired and strengthened, and therefore **not grow weary and lose heart**. No-one is more encouraging than Jesus, but the role of witnesses in encouraging other believers is not to be under-estimated either.

We can remember that the English word 'to encourage' means to give courage to someone, just as the word 'to hearten' means to give heart, and that these are the antidotes to the malaise of losing heart. By God's grace we shall be known as encouragers, part of the **great cloud of witnesses**. The metaphor of a 'cloud' was probably suggested by allusion to the thought of resurrected believers rising through the clouds in their ascension to heaven. If one looks up to heaven, then the saints and angels are in or above the clouds.

Hebrews uses a metaphor for living as a believer which is a favourite in the New Testament. He speaks about it as a **race** in which we are running (see 1 Cor. 9:24; Gal. 2:2 and 2 Tim. 2:5). When you are running in a race you need to get rid of handicaps which will slow you down. To travel far or fast you need to travel light. In the same way we are advised in our pilgrimage of faith to **throw off everything that hinders**.

The expression used here refers to excessive loads or real burdens. For each of us we will have to discern what burdens are weighing us down: guilt that should have been dealt with, fear of change, peer pressure, aspects of our culture which are not appropriate for gospel life, patterns of living which have become too strong, etc.

Just as an athlete will want to be free of any clothing or baggage which interferes with smooth running, so *Hebrews* advises us to get rid of **the sin that so easily entangles**. This may be a reference to a specific sin which characterised those to whom *Hebrews* was writing, but in the context it probably means whatever sin bedevils each of us. Unless we deal with sin as and when it occurs in our lives, then it will trip us up just as we are running well in the race of life.

If we do sort out our lives under the Lord's leading and grace, then we will be able to **run with perseverance the race marked out for us**. The witnesses of chapter 11 have already run their race and can testify that the hard work and persecution are worth it. Now it is our turn to set our sights on the finishing line, as it were, and 'tough it out' for the sake of our witness to the Lord. The word translated **perseverance** is one which is used a few times by *Hebrews* in the closing part of this pastoral letter (10:32, 36; 12:7).

It is not the word for grudging or defeated resignation when people simply grit their teeth and bear it, nor does it convey the idea of keeping one's head down and waiting for things to pass. It is a term for the attitude which is determined to defeat the obstacles that come its way, taking however long it takes, but always convinced that victory can be won. There is a kind of confidence which is inappropriate for believers, since we are dependent on the Lord for our lives, and our confidence, in that sense, should be in the Lord alone. But having said that, there is also a kind of confidence which the Lord wishes to give us and to nurture in us, helping us to be able to face life and act as people who belong to the Lord.

So we determine to run our race with endurance, and **fix our eyes on Jesus**. This verb means to be aware of other things to look at, distractions and temptations, and yet to deliberately focus on Jesus to the exclusion of all else. He is the absolute inspiration for us, **the author and perfecter of our faith**. The term for **author** is translated in other versions as 'pioneer', and this perhaps conveys the meaning in a better way. It is the same word as was used in *Hebrews* 2:10, and reference can be made to the discussion there. Keeping alive the context here of the racing metaphor, Jesus has blazed the trail for us to follow in life and death, and also through resurrection to eternal life.

Calling him the **perfecter of our faith** employs the term which we have seen before in *Hebrews* for making things complete. Necessary as our faith, integrity and service are, and important as encouragements from others are, only Jesus ran the full race, and only he can fulfil our lives. Only he **endured the cross, scorning its shame**. It is interesting to note that although the cross and its shame are always in the mind of *Hebrews* throughout the letter, this is the only place where they are actually mentioned.

Hebrews is determined to let his readers know that they are not alone in their experience of persecution for the sake of the Lord. Some of them may become martyrs for the Lord, but even Jesus died at the hands of men, and he experienced an alienation on the cross which they will never know. The possibility of martyrdom was a real one in that generation, and *Hebrews* is not afraid to raise the subject with those he loves so much, as we see in verse 4. To even point out that they have **not yet** been put to the ultimate test was to set them thinking about the possibility to come.

Jesus endured all that he did **for the joy set before him** — the joy of making salvation possible for all people, the joy of sitting **at the right hand of the throne of God**, and the joy of preparing a place in heaven for his people (John 14:1-3). We who follow Jesus are to consider the joy set before us to enable us to finish running the hard race, and so as not to **grow weary and lose heart**. At the end of this section of the letter *Hebrews* returns to this theme of not giving up. He says **strengthen your feeble arms and weak knees**.

Being considerate for those for whom the race is particularly difficult – **the lame** – we are to **make level paths** for one another. Note again the way that *Hebrews* keeps reminding us of the importance of taking care of one another in the family of the Messiah.

The two expressions translated as growing weary and losing heart are actually used in classical Greek to describe athletes who either fall to the ground or throw themselves on the ground in utter exhaustion after they have crossed the finishing line. In other words, *Hebrews* is continuing to use this wonderfully apt metaphor of a race to say to his readers that they must not give up too soon. They must not admit defeat, but rather stay on their feet until they have finished the race. Then, as *Hebrews* has said already in 4:1-11, will come the time for rest and restoration.

These words naturally take us back to the prophetic teaching of Isaiah where he also encourages us to trust in the Lord who will enable us to keep going with renewed strength and joy:

He gives strength to the weary and increases the power of the weak. Even youths grow tired and weary, and young men stumble and fall; but those who hope in the LORD will renew their strength. They will soar on wings like eagles; they will run and not grow weary, they will walk and not be faint (Isa. 40:29-31).

The other major emphasis in this section is on the **word of encouragement** to see suffering in life in a more positive vein, namely as an experience of discipline from the Lord. This perspective is reinforced by *Hebrews* with his quoting of Proverbs 3:11-12 and its further encouragement to see the Lord's discipline as evidence of the Lord's love for his people. He is urging them to **endure hardship as discipline**.

We might see it in the following way: a father who did not love his young son might ignore behaviour or attitudes which he knew would lead to difficulties in his son's adult life, and a superficial analysis of the relationship might decide that that father loved his son and gave him complete freedom to live his own life. However, an immature son might well make bad choices about his life and a loving father will be prepared to discipline his son even if it put a strain on the relationship from time to time.

In this sense the Lord shows his genuine love for his people by not shrinking back from the responsibility of discipline. It serves to purify and strengthen those who are disciplined if they can accept it in good grace. *Hebrews* says that it **produces a harvest of righteousness and peace** for such people. Indeed, he returns to the athletic metaphor which he has used so well in this section and states that those who *can* see hardship as discipline are **trained by it**.

The word translated as **trained** comes from the root which gives us the word 'gymnastics' in English. To be trained thoroughly is to work hard and to be pushed hard by one's coach. If we might be so bold as to say so, Jesus is the coach of believers, and in the end the effort is well worth while as we finish the race and rest with him for eternity. The point is that **everyone undergoes discipline** in one way or another, and therefore we need to choose how we will see it and respond. The word translated here by **undergoes** is the one used in *Hebrews* 3:1 for sharing or participating in something, and reference can be made to the discussion there.

Finally, we must note the significance of the strong language used by *Hebrews* when he says that those who refuse the lessons of discipline, and therefore **are not disciplined**,

are **illegitimate children**. Although this term can be used in
Hebrew as a term of contempt, just as the word 'bastard' can
in English, it does not have the same meaning in the two
cultures and languages. In English law it refers to someone
born out of wedlock, and therefore 'illegitimate children' is a
phrase which makes sense to English readers.

In Jewish law, however, the term is different altogether
and refers to someone who is the child of a marriage, which
was prohibited in Jewish religious law. We see the basis of
this set of laws in Leviticus 18, and there are serious legal and
social implications for the children of such forbidden
marriages. For example, a mamzer, to use the Hebrew term,
cannot marry any Jewish person. In order to marry a Jewish
woman, say, a male mamzer would have to convert to Judaism
first of all so that in effect two Jewish people were being
married.

This particular example has become a serious issue in
contemporary Israel where all marriages have to come under
the supervision of the Orthodox Jewish authorities. When a
marriage (authorised outside of Israel has involved a woman
who was not Jewish, or who was converted under non-
Orthodox authority) has produced a child who later
immigrated to become an Israeli citizen and has then applied
to marry a Jewish Israeli, then the Orthodox authorities have
ruled such an application illegal. This situation arises regularly,
if not overly frequently.

And so, the point which *Hebrews* is making, as a Jewish
believer writing to Jewish believers, is that anyone who refuses
the godly benefit of discipline is not really a full member of
the community, but an outsider. Such a person might well
have to start again to be accepted into the community of faith
if they repent of their previous hardness of heart. They are
not true sons.

To accept hardship as discipline from the Lord is to accept

the fullness of his love, and so to be in the proper relationship with him. It is almost as if *Hebrews* is saying that to belong properly to the Bride of the Messiah, using the marriage metaphor of Ephesians 5 and Revelation 21 and 22, one needs to be receiving discipline in the right way for it to be a legitimate marriage. Love, in one sense, is not enough in itself. Successful marriages are worked on, as well as being based on love, and a proper 'marriage' between believers and the Lord also requires persistence and a determination to face hardships with and for the Lord.

35. Therefore we dare not treat God lightly (A) (12:14-29)

This is a particularly striking passage in the letter, and in it *Hebrews* employs one last great contrasting image – that of the two towering mountains of the Hebrew Bible, **Sinai** and **Zion**. Other passages where he has used this method of teaching by contrasting are 1:4-14; 2:1-4; 2:5-9; 3:1-6; 3:7-4:11; 5:1-10; 8:1-5; 8:6-13; 9:1-5; 9:6-14. Here he introduces to his readers the symbol of the revelation of God's will to his people after the Exodus, and the symbol of God's sovereign reign among his people in the temple. The first lays down the ground rules for life in the Kingdom of God and the second looks forward to the coming of the Messiah who will reign from Jerusalem in the Messianic Age.

In *Hebrews*, Sinai is taken as representative of the life of the people of God before the coming of Jesus, whereas Zion speaks of the **heavenly Jerusalem**, now transformed, as it were, by the residence there of the risen Lord Jesus. We shall return to this in a moment. Sinai was a genuine place of **the living God**, however, for Israel met with God there (Exod. 19:16-20; 20:18-21; Deut. 4:10-13). This language is the background to *Hebrews* 12:21, and so we know that Sinai was in his mind.

The theophany at Sinai, the appearance of God there, was

accompanied by 'fire', 'smoke', 'thick cloud' and 'thunder and lightning', which explains the references to **burning with fire, darkness, gloom** and **storm**. In fact these 'natural phenomena' were commonly associated with the appearance of the Lord (see Exod. 13:21; Judg. 13:20; 1 Kgs. 18:38; Gen. 15:12; Exod. 10:21-22; 14:20; 1 Kgs. 8:12; Amos 5:18; Job 37:9; 38:1; Nah. 1:3; Zech. 9:14).

At Sinai there was also 'a very loud trumpet blast', meaning by this the blast of the shofar, or ram's horn, still used today by the Jewish community, notably at the time of Rosh HaShanah and Yom Kippur. This explains the reference to **a trumpet blast** in *Hebrews*. This sound will also be heard at the time of the climax of history (see Isa. 27:13; Zech. 9:14; Matt. 24:31; 1 Cor. 15:52; 1 Thess. 4:16).

The voice of God had thundered in the ears and hearts of the people at Sinai, the very mountain had trembled, and everyone, including Moses, was afraid. It was even too much to listen to God's voice (Exod. 20:18-19)! The time and place were so **holy**, which is to say set apart for the presence and purpose of God, that even to touch the mountain was to face death (Exod. 19:12-13). It is important to note, therefore, that in spite of the contrast which *Hebrews* is making, he never loses sight of the fact that a holy fear is still appropriate even in the time of the new revelation in Jesus. We shall return to this shortly.

Mount Zion was the mountain where King David brought the Ark of the Covenant, the symbol of God's presence and purpose, and so gave the place its great importance (2 Sam. 6:1-19). It became forever associated with both the presence of God as Israel's King and the presence of the Messiah, David's greater son. *Hebrews* shares this vision of **the heavenly Jerusalem** (here and at 11:10, 13-16 and 13:14) with John (Rev. 21:2) and Paul (Gal. 4:24-26). In John's great vision, he saw Jesus standing there on Mount Zion (Rev. 14:1).

Within the contrast of the two mountains and what they represent, we also have the contrast presented as to the difference between the words of Moses and those of Jesus. Moses was the mediator of the covenant sealed at Sinai, and the word used to say that he **warned** the people implies that he was a channel of words which came from someone else. The use of Moses as a speaker is what is meant by saying that the people were warned **on earth**. And yet that was serious enough that those who chose to ignore a mere mouthpiece, as it were, **did not escape** the wrath of God.

When *Hebrews* in this same passage uses a word for Jesus, who **speaks** to us as **the mediator of a new covenant**, he uses a term which implies direct speech. Jesus' words are the words of God, and therefore how much more serious must it be to ignore him when he **warns us from heaven**! Mount Sinai was significant enough, and it stands in the way of anyone who tries to live his/her own life while paying lip-service to God's authority and grace. But Mount Zion, the home of the risen Jesus, is even more significant, and defines those who belong to the true community of God's faithful people.

All of this thinking about the presence of God causing the mountain and the people to tremble, and the voice of God making people shake with fear, leads *Hebrews* to present another image of the seriousness of taking God lightly when he speaks. When the Lord spoke on Sinai 'the whole mountain trembled violently'. The Psalms speak often of this display of awesome power from the Lord:

When you went out before your people, O God ... the earth shook ... (Ps. 68:7-8).

Your thunder was heard in the whirlwind ... the earth trembled and quaked ... (Ps. 77:18).

Tremble, O earth, at the presence of the Lord ... (Ps. 114:7).

These Psalms all refer to the Sinai event, but *Hebrews* also knows of the shaking of the earth which will happen in the last days. He refers to a passage in the prophets where God says that he will shake up all the nations of the earth (Hag. 2:6). He takes this as a proclamation of the day when the present age will pass away and the new Messianic Age will begin. The coming of Jesus has meant a new level of confrontation between the Kingdom of God and the world in which the devil has power. To stand with Jesus is to experience suffering in the world, just as the whole world is suffering, but to stand with Jesus is to be safe for eternity. All **created things** will be exposed as part of the passing age, with only the Lord and faith in him standing firm.

Those who follow Jesus belong to the world of that which **cannot be shaken**. We are reminded of words right at the start of the letter which also stress that the Lord is the only permanent reality (1:11-12). Because believers belong to Jesus they share in this permanence. **We are receiving a kingdom that cannot be shaken.**

Let us return to the fear which Moses himself felt at the presence of God. As has been said already, it is appropriate to fear the Lord, **for our God is a consuming fire**. It is too easy to dilute the fitting sense of **reverence and awe**, so that it is compromised by a desire to focus on the love and mercy of God. We can be guilty of taking God for granted. *Hebrews* highlights the fact that we should always have a real and active sense of the fear of the Lord to hold in tension with our confidence in the grace and mercy of God, by referring to Moses' own fear of God.

The interesting thing to note is that Moses did not say **I am trembling with fear** when Israel was receiving the Torah at Sinai. He said that when he came down from Sinai and saw that the people whom God loved had committed the sin of creating a golden calf (Deut. 9:15-21). It is the fear of the

Lord, learning never to take him for granted, learning to be grateful for his daily providential care for us, learning to trust and obey him, which is the beginning of real wisdom in life (Prov. 1:7; 9:10).

The community of those who live on Zion is described as a **joyful assembly**. Part of the throng consists of **thousands upon thousands of angels**, and although this may simply be an allusion to the fact that this is **the city of the living God**, so that of course the angels live and praise there, I wonder if more is being said. Jesus taught us that when a sinner repents there is wonderful rejoicing in heaven. Perhaps these angels are rejoicing over those who make the pilgrimage from Sinai to Zion?

These believers are called **the church of the first-born**. Jesus himself is called 'the firstborn over all creation' and 'the firstborn from among the dead' (Col. 1:15, 18). Paul also refers to Jesus as 'the firstborn among many brothers' (Rom. 8:29). In the Hebrew Bible we read that God called Israel his 'firstborn son' (Exod. 4:22), and it is the joy of believers in Jesus to belong to Jesus as a community of children with the promise of blessing befitting the firstborn in God's family.

Being in Jesus' family means that our **names are written in heaven**. Presumably this means that they appear in the register of citizens of heaven, as it were. In Exodus 32:32-33 Moses refers to a 'book' which God has written, and which God refers to as 'my book'. By inference we can see that to be written in the book is to be forgiven for sin and to be welcome in God's presence. We see a reference to a 'book of life' in Psalm 69:28, referring to the righteous people of God. Malachi 3:16 speaks of 'a scroll of remembrance' listing all 'who feared the Lord and honoured his name'. The apocalyptic book of Daniel mentions that everyone 'whose name is found written in the book' will be saved.

In the Pauline letters we find a reference to a 'book of life' in which are written the names of the believers (Phil. 4:3), and this is in addition to six references in John's great vision (Rev. 3:5; 13:8; 17:8; 20:12, 15; 21:27). In two of these last verses it is explicitly stated that this book of life belongs to 'the lamb' of God. Therefore this reference in *Hebrews* is not isolated in Scripture.

The notion of God writing books with the names of those who are to live and to die, to receive a good year or a bad year, has become a fundamental one in Judaism. It is one of the focal points in the spirituality of the 10 Days of Awe between Rosh HaShanah (the Jewish New Year) and Yom Kippur (the Day of Atonement). The belief is that God opens these heavenly books on Rosh HaShanah and seals them shut at the close of Yom Kippur, with people's names written in either the book of life or the other book. We have enough references to the books of heaven in Jewish and early Christian literature of the period surrounding the time of Jesus to infer that it was a common belief even then.

Hebrews uses this belief to underline the importance of being written in the book of life in heaven. This is vital because Zion is also the home of **God the judge of all men**. There is no way to avoid facing up to God with the testimony of our lives. We find the connection of judgment with the book of life also spelled out in Revelation 20:11-15. In the same way that the book of life and salvation belongs to Jesus, it is to be remembered that judgment has also been entrusted to Jesus by the Father (John 5:21-22).

In Revelation 13 and 21 this book of life is said to be written by the lamb, and for most believers this would conjure up an image of a kind, gentle and loving animal, very well suited to the ministry of saving and sustaining. Yet this is not the whole story at all, and even in Revelation we read the startling words that in the days of judgment people will be terrified of 'the wrath of the lamb' (6:16). This is not an image which we find natural or comfortable. We dare not take the Lord for granted!

What we must do is **be thankful** to God and **worship God acceptably with reverence and awe**. The word translated as 'worship' is one of the basic words in the New Testament which is used to translate the Hebrew term for the worship of God. The root Hebrew and Jewish concept of worship is especially rich and surprising to many believers today. The Hebrew root is the very one for the common term for 'work' or 'service'. To work in the garden or in the office, etc. one uses the same word as for worshipping God.

This does not mean that in the Hebrew Bible and Jewish community life worship is just hard work and not a joyful, liberating experience. On the contrary, the worship of God is an attitude and activity, as it were, which explodes in praise and thanksgiving. What is being communicated by the use of this word, however, is that worship is far more than praise. It is not to be limited by or affected by our moods, in the sense that we only really worship God when we feel joyful, or the like.

There is a definite dimension of responsibility and service of God in all situations which is at the heart of what the Bible calls the authentic worship of God. God is our Lord, and we are his servants. Obedience is therefore a fundamental aspect of true worship. God has a 'right' to our worship, and it is not a matter of whether or not we feel in the mood to worship him or not. It is an attitude for the whole of life, and is not to be defined merely in terms of special times and places of worship.

Indeed some translations of the Bible often translate the original word by 'service' as well as often using the word 'worship'. They will also often speak of 'the servants of the Lord' as well as 'those who worship the Lord'. The point is extremely important: when we serve the Lord in any capacity, as long as our hearts are right before God and we are performing the service willingly, then that service is an expression of our worship. In the context of this *Hebrews* passage, we are being taught that a proper fear of the Lord and a determination to walk in a godly way before him are necessary aspects of the 'acceptable' worship of God.

36. Therefore we dare not treat God lightly (B) (12:14-29)

As we seek to serve and worship the Lord in accordance with his will, we are urged to **make every effort** to behave in certain ways. This is not a denial of the central role of God's grace in our lives, nor an encouragement to develop some sort of 'works' righteousness', but rather a focus on the fact that we do have responsibility to serve God within our relationship with him.

We are **to live in peace** with everyone. As we know, the concept of 'shalom' which lies behind this word for peace means much more than the absence of hostility. It is the expression for a wholeness of life and relationships, for real harmony in life, for a desire to see others fulfilled in life. We are reminded of the words of the Psalmist when he urges us to 'seek peace, and pursue it' (Ps. 34:14). *Hebrews* does not simply say that we are to look forward to experiencing this shalom of God in our lives. We are to **make every effort** to have that kind of relationship with one another and, as the Psalmist puts it, pursue it in life. Jesus himself said that the 'sons of God' are those who seek to make peace, not those who wish for it or simply enjoy it themselves (Matt. 5:9).

Paul also encourages us to 'live at peace with everyone' in Romans 12:18, but his context is even more specific. He is teaching there that we should be so like Jesus that we overcome the natural desire for revenge on those who do us harm, and prefer to bless them and develop a relationship of shalom with them (verses 17-21). This context may not have been absent from the mind of *Hebrews* as he wrote in a situation where the believers were undergoing persecution for their faith in Jesus. It is a challenge for all believers.

Secondly, we are encouraged **to be holy**. As has been pointed out before, the root idea here is that of being distinct from the world and common use. Believers are not to share the world's standards or ideals. Only those who really seek to serve and worship the Lord with their lives, following him in all things, separating themselves from the ways of the world and devoting themselves positively to personal holiness will **see the Lord**.

Therefore it is imperative that we realise that the ideal life for believers is not one in which we simply lie back and let the Lord do all the work. Total passivity is not there as an option for a mature follower of Jesus. We are called to a life of self-discipline in which we are struggling daily to keep focused on the Lord and to be crucifying the flesh. But more than this, we are also called to be making sure that we are taking care of one another in God's family.

See to it that no-one misses the grace of God, says *Hebrews*. The word used here for 'misses' is one which was used in Greek to describe those on a march who straggled behind everyone for so long that they were finally left behind. This is a vivid picture of our mutual responsibility. We are called to be constantly looking out for one another, making sure that no-one drifts away from the body of marchers in God's company. The grace of God will always lead us on and we have to keep up with him.

Hebrews goes on to alert the community to another danger, and therefore another responsibility. **See to it that ... no bitter root grows up to cause trouble and defile many**. Here we have an obvious reference to a text in Deuteronomy 29:17 (verse 18 in the translation), part of a passage describing the effects on the community of anyone who abandons the pure worship of the Lord and commits idolatry, urging others to commit the same sin. Moses says to the people in that context, 'make sure there is no root among you that produces such bitter poison'.

This is a warning from *Hebrews* against those whom he knows would have a strong corrupting influence on the community of the faithful. *Hebrews* has just encouraged his people **to live in peace** with each other, but this peace will be subverted by any who spread a message of compromise with the world and its values. In the passage from Deuteronomy which is alluded to here, those who tried to follow other gods and to 'hedge their bets', as it were, made the mistake of thinking that they would have peace in their lives as a result of it.

In Deuteronomy 29:18 (verse 19 in the translation), they deceive themselves by thinking, 'I will have peace' (translated in the NIV as, 'I will be safe'). The truth is, however, that the Lord is a jealous God, and he will not allow that compromising of his authority and relationship with his people to go unpunished.

If we keep these last two warnings in *Hebrews* together, we see that he is alerting his people to the fact that it is often those who do seem to lose sight of the wonderful grace of God, for whatever reason, who feel the need to bolster their lack of relationship with the Lord with other sources of security or satisfaction. We really do have a serious obligation to care for one another in the family of God!

A further warning seems to be quite straightforward: **see that no-one is sexually immoral**. Scripture is full of warnings against various types of sexual immorality. We are brought back to this issue in 13:4, and it will be discussed there. And then comes a more complex issue: **see that no-one is ... godless like Esau**. The word translated as 'godless' is one which described land which was used for profane purposes, in distinction to being used for sacred purposes. The same word was also employed for people who were completely lacking in a sense of awe-full devotion to God, and who lived life as if the visible world was all that there was.

Esau is held in Jewish tradition to be an example of such a person. He was not able to see beyond the immediate, and therefore he was not able to exercise discipline and devotion to God. Therefore he **sold his inheritance rights** to his brother, perhaps assuming or hoping that he could still receive his inheritance in some way.

But once the blessing had been given to Jacob there was nothing which could be done to undo the damage of the missed inheritance. Repentance is still important for the relationship with God, as it would have been for Esau's relationship with Isaac, if indeed Esau's repentance was genuine, but it may nevertheless be unable to reverse the effects of the lack of faith or devotion to the Lord. *Hebrews* is alerting his readers to the real danger of losing the promised inheritance which God has in store for them.

We see here the pastoral heart of *Hebrews* as he worries about his flock and is at pains to alert them to the many dangers that are only too real in the struggles of life. We cannot have a superficial or triumphalistic view of the nature of life in and for Jesus. The full gospel presentation must take seriously the cost of discipleship in the overall context of the secure love of God in the Messiah, Jesus. In particular we need to remember that this letter was written to a Messianic Jewish community under severe pressure for their faith in Jesus as Israel's one and only Messiah.

For chapter after magnificent chapter *Hebrews* has highlighted all that Jesus has done for them, and then in chapter 11 he painted the famous portrait of heroes and heroines of the faith who bore such effective testimony to the Lord even without having experienced the joy of knowing the Messiah, Jesus. And now in this chapter he teaches his community that the other side of this life of resting in God is the need for self-discipline, for accepting the discipline of God, and for having a healthy fear of the Lord. As he says at the close of the chapter, **our God is a consuming fire**.

37. We are called to care for those in need of care (13:1-3)

As *Hebrews* begins to draw his letter to a close, he emphasises the importance of love and generosity in binding a community together and providing a basis for reaching others. He opens by urging a genuine love for the **brothers**. Literally, he says, 'let brotherly love continue', using the Greek term *philadelphia*, the very term which was chosen as the name of the famous city in the USA.

It is possible that what is in mind here is a love and commitment to other believers. Both Paul and Peter use this term in contexts which definitely suggest that they have believers in mind (Rom. 12:10; 1 Pet. 1:22). We have already been told in *Hebrews* 2:11-12 that Jesus himself calls believers his 'brothers', and *Hebrews* also calls them his 'holy brothers' (3:1). It is very possible that there were threats of divisions within that community (e.g. see 12:14; 13:9), so that this exhortation to express the Father's love to one another was rooted in potential trouble rather than simply being a good piece of advice.

But the full exhortation is to **keep on loving** the community of believers. The love which is appropriate for those who follow Jesus and his example of love is not an emotional experience, ebbing and flowing with moods or serious needs. It is an act of commitment to one another, an attitude of generosity and dependability at all times. 1 Corinthians 13:4-7 is an excellent commentary on the nature of the love which *Hebrews* has in mind.

However, it is also possible for believers in a community

to be so caught up with one another that they fail to keep involved in any active engagement with others. The world needs to know the love of God, and we must share it with them, not only with each other in the family of God. Therefore *Hebrews* goes on immediately to say to his readers, **do not forget to entertain strangers**. The literal translation would be not to forget 'love of strangers'.

The word for 'strangers' was commonly used to describe people who were held to be real outsiders to a community. It gives the English language its word 'xenophobia' for fear of, and usually hatred of foreigners. *Hebrews* is speaking here about the need for a genuinely generous attitude towards strangers, a measure of hospitality which would bear a strong witness to the love of the Lord. The Jewish community then, as now, took hospitality very seriously, and indeed it was regarded as a high virtue by most in the world of that time.

Strangers who might stay with believers would include other believers on the move as well as non-believers. At a time when many of the institutional inns were likely to be dangerous, immoral or extremely expensive, the act of welcoming someone to stay in a house dedicated to serving Jesus would be a real service. *Hebrews* goes on to say that by so doing we might become like those who have **entertained angels without knowing it**. Presumably he is thinking of passages in Scripture like Genesis 18:1-19 and Judges 13.

Of course Jesus taught that to welcome and care for others is to welcome and care for him (Matt. 25:31-40), and as we saw at the start of this letter, Jesus is far superior to the angels! The point which Jesus is making is that we are not to judge people and care only for those whom we know and like, or those who are like us in some way, or those who will repay the kindness: rather we are to show the same love to strangers and those who are not like us, for in this way we are looking for Jesus in each person.

Hebrews' point is that angels are those beings whom God
sometimes uses to communicate to us. The word in Hebrew
for an angel simply means 'a messenger'. It is only by opening
ourselves to others that we can discover whether they have
something to teach us about life with the Lord. This point
retains its force whether we think that *Hebrews* is referring to
real angels in this passage or whether we think that he is using
the term more generally to mean people chosen by God to be
his messengers to us. And let us not limit such people to other
believers. Sometimes the Lord speaks to us through the
questions or attitudes of non-believers.

Hebrews immediately proceeds to encourage his people to
remember those in prison ... and those who are ill-treated.
What is more, he encourages this love in action to stem not
from an intellectual knowledge that such care is right, but
from a sense of real fellow-feeling – **as if you were their
fellow prisoners ... as if you yourselves were suffering**. This
reflects a distinctively Jewish attitude to care for others. Those
who have suffered and know what it is to be grateful to the
Lord for deliverance should have an active compassion for
others who are suffering.

For example, in Deuteronomy 5:12-15 we read that the
Israelites are to keep the Sabbath as a sacred day before the
Lord, and that all their servants and livestock, and even
strangers who are in their homes, are to be given the joy of
that Sabbath rest as well. Note the reference to strangers in
the Deuteronomy passage. And if anyone asks why this day
should be kept, and why the servants, etc. should also be given
this privilege, then the answer is that the Israelites are to

Remember that you were slaves in Egypt and that the LORD your
God brought you out of there with a mighty hand and an
outstretched arm. Therefore the LORD your God has commanded
you to observe the Sabbath day (Deut. 5:15).

Evangelists and believers with a strong desire to share their faith with others will testify to the power of this attitude in their own motivation. To remember one's own life before becoming a believer in Jesus and to be truly grateful to the Lord for making all the difference in one's life provide a constant impetus to want to help others to share the same experience. Believers who have a real testimony of God's grace in their lives are not judgmental about the lives of others, but want to do whatever they can to help.

More specifically, it may be that the suffering people whom *Hebrews* has in mind are believers who are in prison as a result of their faith in Jesus. This would anchor their fellow-feeling in an appreciation of the fact that in a short time they too could be in that very position of suffering. Most believers reading this commentary are far from likely to be put in prison or to be made to really suffer for their faith, but it is vital that we all realise that we have brothers and sisters in the Lord today who are facing this possibility.

In fact many have been martyred in the second half of this century, let alone in previous generations. For sizeable numbers of people the cost of discipleship for following Jesus might well include the possibility of death. And quite apart from martyrdom, many have suffered terrible torture, exile, imprisonment, loss of jobs, family and all friends as a direct result of their profession of faith in Jesus as Lord.

In the light of our comfortable lives it is probably more necessary for western believers today than for believers in other parts of the world, let alone the original recipients of *Hebrews'* letter to heed the call to **remember those in prison ... and those who are ill-treated**.

38. We must beware immorality, greed and lack of trust in God (13:4-6)

Hebrews says something which at first glance might seem to be simply a warning against adultery. He actually states that **the marriage bed** must be **kept pure** and that **God will judge the adulterer,** but there is more going on here than this. If we begin here, though, then we see that *Hebrews* is simply insisting on the moral standards which are clear throughout Scripture. He also reminds his readers that God will judge **all the sexually immoral**.

One of the most powerful aspects of testimony of the new community of believers in Jesus which we know from pagan writers in the early decades and centuries to have made a huge impact on society was the commitment to a highly moral lifestyle. In this context, sexual morality was a fundamental area in need of a revolutionary change, and faithfulness within marriage was an indispensable dimension of this. It is surely exactly the same in our own society!

However there is another possible reference here which would have been just as important in that day and age. Many religiously devoted people were despairing of the state of humanity and were preparing themselves for the imminent end of the world which they felt sure could not be too far away. As part of their severe programme of self-discipline and devotion to God they rejected the possibility of marriage, having children and engaging in family life.

This kind of radical asceticism is not a virtue in Scripture, and it may be that *Hebrews* was pleading for believers to go on establishing families and homes for the hospitality which he has just been commending in 13:1-3. The human body and the enjoyment of a healthy and morally upright sexual relationship with one's marriage partner are not evil in themselves – far from it – although there is no doubt that they can be horribly abused. Our society also needs good role models of marriages and homes from those who follow Jesus.

One more point which needs to be raised here is that all of the above comments would seem to have been relatively unnecessary when writing to a community of Jewish believers in Jesus. The Jewish community as a whole was not only very well aware of the importance of sexual morality, especially within marriage relationships, but it was also highly regarded by others for practising what it preached. Surely Jewish believers would have been doubly alert to this without *Hebrews* needing to draw attention to it?

And although full membership of the Jewish community at Qumran may well have involved a pledge of celibacy, with radical asceticism being held up as an ideal, marriage and the bringing of children into the world was then, as now, a positive value for Jewish people. The very first commandment in Scripture, as the rabbis often pointed out, was, 'Be fruitful and increase in number!' (Gen. 1:28). A life of sexual abstinence was not, and is not, a Jewish virtue.

Perhaps, then, some of the believers in *Hebrews'* care had fallen foul of a kind of teaching which had even penetrated the community of believers, trying to present 'the flesh' and everything associated with it as essentially corrupt and corrupting? We know that Paul had to deal with this false teaching when he wrote to Timothy on one occasion:

> The Spirit clearly says that in later times some will abandon the faith and follow deceiving spirits and things taught by demons. Such teachings come through hypocritical liars, whose consciences have been seared as with a hot iron. They forbid people to marry and order them to abstain from certain foods, which God created to be received with thanksgiving by those who believe and who know the truth (1 Tim. 4:1-3).

Intense pressure on believers in society can result in unbalanced lifestyles and unhealthy priorities, and we must be on our guard against this even in our own times. As the year 2000 comes closer in the western calendar and different types of millennial mania emerge with increasing frequency, believers will need to be alert to some subtle and some not so subtle variations on the gospel faith and lifestyle.

Hebrews then moves from the issue of the honour and purity of marriage to the importance of being grateful for the life which God has given us. Greed is an attitude which destroys people, and so he tells his people to stay **free from the love of money**. But this in itself would be to focus on somewhat of a negative intention. To put it positively is much more helpful, and besides, to single out money is merely to highlight the problem of greed. Money in this passage symbolises anything which people might covet to give them a feeling of security or power.

So *Hebrews* expresses the positive attitude which God desires for each of us: **be content with what you have**. John the Baptist understood the value of this, and he was uncompromising when he said to some Roman soldiers that they had to live morally upright lives, before going on to deliver to them the real challenge: 'Be content with your pay' (Luke 3:10-14). Paul learned this lesson himself, and was then able to say, 'I have learned to be content whatever the circumstances' (Phil. 4:11).

The matter which is uppermost in *Hebrews'* mind is probably that it is human nature to seek security in times of pressure or fear. But these believers need to learn to trust in God to take care of them. Even if they feel vulnerable compared to others, it is vital that they put their faith into practice. Therefore *Hebrews* reminds them of two passages in the Hebrew Bible which encourage trust in God in spite of what seem to be overwhelming obstacles (Josh. 1:6-9; Ps. 118:6-7).

The same message is as applicable to believers today as it was then! (See also Matt. 6:19-34; Phil. 4:6, 11-13, 19; 1 Tim. 6:6-10, 17-19).

39. We must honour our leaders under God (13:7, 17)

Although these two verses do not follow one another
consecutively in the chapter, it makes sense to deal with them
together since they cover the same issue. Three verses in this
final chapter mention 'leaders' (7,17,24), and combined with
verse 18 they give the impression that *Hebrews* is referring to
leaders of the community who are with the community at the
time that he is separated from them. We certainly seem to be
reading material which would have been appropriate for the
closing section of a letter. None of this implies in any way
that *Hebrews* was not considered a leader of the community
as well, and in fact the whole tone and content of the letter
make it clear that he had massive authority, even while
separated from them.

In verse 7 *Hebrews* encourages his readers to **remember
your leaders**. This might simply be a challenge to keep them
in mind constantly. However, when combined with the next
clause in which they are spoken of in the past tense – **who
spoke the word of God to you** – it could suggest that those
particular leaders are dead.

We might only have a past reference for the reason that
Hebrews is alluding to a time in the past when those leaders
first spoke the word of God to the people who have since
become believers. But it is certainly possible, and in keeping
with the context of the letter, to surmise that these leaders
may already have become victims of persecution. They might
have died in terms of *Hebrews* 12:4. If this is the case, then
the leaders referred to in verse 17 (and also in verse 24) must
be a different set of leaders.

Therefore many commentators prefer to think of the leaders
in verse 7 as being still alive, with *Hebrews* simply taking his
people's minds back to the first days of their faith. In any
case, the readers are to **consider the outcome of their way**

of life and imitate their faith. After the splendour and challenge of chapter 11 with its heroes and heroines of faith *Hebrews* still returns to the present and holds up the current leaders as worthy models of faith. This is a sobering responsibility for leaders who follow Jesus.

Paul had the courage to hold himself up as a model for others to imitate:

> Follow my example, as I follow the example of the Messiah (1 Cor. 11:1).

The word used by *Hebrews* which is translated by 'consider' means 'to pay very close attention'. They were to examine the 'outcome' of their lives and copy their faith. This 'outcome' could mean the unshakable faith which they showed in their lives, and/or the moral testimony of their lifestyles. It is a challenge, in this case, to live lives which bring honour to the name of Jesus, and it sits easily with the previous verses in the chapter.

On the other hand, if it is right to see here a reference to leaders who had been martyred in a time of persecution, it could mean that the readers were being urged to take inspiration from the way in which those leaders met their deaths with faith. This would then give a profound depth to the encouragement to **imitate their faith**. It was a time and culture when people were terrified of death and what lay beyond it, and the testimony of believers meeting death with courage, confidence and hope would have been a tremendous witness to the new faith.

What must not be missed in this verse is the assumption of the quality of the lives of those in leadership in the community of believers. Because this is the case, it would have been even easier for them to receive what *Hebrews* went on to urge in verse 17 when he told his readers to **obey your leaders and submit to their authority**. Accepting and respecting authority is a biblical charge to believers, but there is no doubt that it comes easier when that authority is exercised in godly ways by godly leaders.

The New Testament does not advocate blind obedience to spiritual leaders, and that is not what is in *Hebrews'* mind at this point. He has said in verse 9 that his readers need to be discerning about what is taught; John tells us to test all spirits (1 John 4:1); Paul stresses the need for an attitude which will produce a mutual desire for believers to honour the other more than they do themselves (e.g. Rom. 12:10; Gal. 5:13; Eph. 5:21; Phil. 2:3-4); and both Paul and Peter know that to be a good leader you need to be modest and considerate of others (e.g. 1 Tim. 5:1-2; Tit. 1:7-8; 1 Pet. 5:1-5).

However, leadership is godly, and the Lord has decreed from the very beginning that there should be leaders among his people. The teaching and pastoral authority of our spiritual leaders is to be respected and accepted. This is the normal situation of the community of believers, and only when there is serious doubt about the soundness of a person's life or teaching is it to be ignored or challenged.

If believers are constantly challenging their leaders or simply ignoring them and going their own way in life then the call to leadership becomes a frustration and a burden. *Hebrews* says that leaders are to be obeyed **so that their work will be a joy, not a burden**. This last word is actually a Greek word which is a strong term for 'groaning'. When congregational pastors or elders, or believers in other areas of leadership, for example missionary societies or ministry training centres, experience their role as a bitter or thankless one then not only is that a terrible shame for those people who have been called by God into those roles, but it will bring a loss of direction, confidence and fellowship to the whole congregation, etc.

This is what *Hebrews* is saying when he states that such a

situation of frustrated leadership **would be of no advantage
to you**. Sadly, we are now living in an age when large numbers
of believers find it difficult to accept the concept of any
spiritual leadership. Many are convinced that our fellowships
and congregations are not nearly as strong as they should be
because of this lack of proper cohesion and integration under
anointed leadership.

The other side of this, of course, is that leaders are
commanded to lead in ways which honour the Lordship of
Jesus. Leaders will answer to the Lord for the way in which
they have led the believers over whom they were given
authority and responsibility. As *Hebrews* puts it, they must
watch over their people, and they must do this knowing that
they will **give an account** to God.

James gives us a sharp reminder of this context of the
accountability of leaders in his famous word about teachers:

> Not many of you should presume to be teachers, my brothers,
> because you know that we who teach will be judged more strictly
> (Jas. 3:1).

In our passage in *Hebrews*, the focus is on the pastoral care of
believers. The term for 'watching over' was used for shepherds
guarding their sheep and taking care of their needs for pasture.
It was also used for soldiers on sentry duty. Indeed this very
term was used in the Septuagint's books of the prophets to
translate the word for watchmen guarding the city walls (Isa.
62:6; Ezek. 3:17; 33:1-9).

The two passages from Ezekiel are particularly appropriate
here, since the Lord makes it clear to the prophet that if he
fails in his duty to guard and alert the people then the Lord
will hold him accountable. All spiritual leaders are advised to
take those words to heart. But it would have been especially
appropriate at that time of real problems for the believers.
They needed watchmen on the walls, and the community is
urged to co-operate lovingly with their leaders.

40. We must fix our faith on the Lord's grace and permanence (13:8-14)

This section opens with one of the best known proclamations in the entire New Testament, and we should begin by noting the significance of it coming here in the letter. In verse 7 we have reference to the godly leadership of those who are called to give examples of faith and lifestyle to believers, and in verse 9 we are warned about false teachers who will lead the faithful astray if allowed. What is fundamental is the need to keep our eyes firmly fixed on Jesus so that we can discern the truth (see 12:2).

Jesus is constant and the gospel is also constant, as verse 8 teaches, and so we are to be alert to **all kinds of strange teachings** which people will come up with from time to time. Paul had to give the same warning to Timothy:

> For the time will come when men will not put up with sound doctrine. Instead, to suit their own desires, they will gather around them a great number of teachers to say what their itching ears want to hear. They will turn their ears away from the truth and turn aside to myths (2 Tim. 4:3-4).

Hebrews was especially concerned by a particular type of false teaching which was threatening to confuse and upset these Jewish believers. He pleads for them to understand that their **hearts** are to be **strengthened by grace**. This is the spiritual food that they need – to know that the Lord has won the victory on their behalf by his death on the cross.

And yet the clear implication is that there were others who were maintaining that there was a need for **ceremonial foods** as well, even although *Hebrews* is in no doubt that these foods are **of no value** whatsoever. The Jewish community lived with very strict food laws, both for everyday life and also for the preparation of the sacrifices in the temple. We see many of these food laws set out in Leviticus 11. But it is the temple rather than the home which is in mind here.

Perhaps there were certain Jewish believers who went beyond simply saying that Jewish believers were entitled to keep their Jewish food laws as an authentic expression of their Jewishness? Perhaps these others were trying to insist that keeping the various ceremonial food laws in particular was a necessary condition for their salvation and membership in the family of the Messiah? Or perhaps they were teaching that the keeping of these laws would make them stronger believers?

Hebrews has already dealt with this type of theology in 9:10. It was not uncommon to find this serious debate going on among Jewish believers, as we see also from Colossians 2:16-17. There is but one sacrifice which counts for believers – the death of Jesus for our salvation. Whereas Jewish believers can keep the laws of kashrut if they so choose, that is not the issue in this passage. The issue is the offering of sacrifices by believers, and *Hebrews* says that there is no spiritual value to be gained from wishing to carry on with that system of sacrifices. Jesus' death, once and for all, has become the last word on that subject.

For other Jewish people, those who do not believe in Jesus, there is still a perceived need to put their trust in the sacrifices. But **those who minister at the tabernacle**, as *Hebrews* calls the priests, are missing the true sacrifice. There is a huge gulf between the reality of Jesus' atoning death and the work of others, and we are told that these others **have no right to eat** at the commemoration of the Lord's sacrifice.

The **altar** to which *Hebrews* refers is the metaphorical altar on which Jesus was sacrificed. We also have an allusion here to the religious tradition among both Jewish and other people for the person bringing certain sacrifices to receive part of the sacrificed animal back for a ceremonial family meal. This is not at all what happens at the commemoration service known as the Lord's Supper, Communion, or the Eucharist.

At the Lord's Supper believers gather to remember and give thanks for what Jesus did for us. The eating of the bread and the drinking of the wine are not a taking away from the sacrificed portion of the sacrificed animal, as it were, but a symbolic participation with Jesus in his death and resurrection (see John 6:25-59). The Communion Service is not a sacrifice, nor in fact an offering of any kind by believers but rather a time for believers to receive from the Lord.

Non-believers should not be invited or allowed to participate in this service, since they have not committed themselves to the worship and service of Jesus. It is the Lord's people, saved by grace, who gather to receive at the Lord's table.

Hebrews carries on with his image of sacrifice. He mentions the **sin offering** and relates this to Jesus' death in two ways. First of all, the high priest carried the **blood** of the animal sacrificed as a sin offering **into the Most Holy Place**, just as Jesus had to shed his blood **to make the people holy**. Secondly, the **bodies** were taken to be **burned outside the camp**, pointing to Jesus' death **outside the city gate** (Lev. 4:12. See also Lev. 16:27 for the same commandment concerning the Day of Atonement).

But there is even more to this imagery of being taken out of the city gate than that of the sin offering. It also recalls the shame of ritual impurity shared by lepers and others who had to stay outside the camp of the Israelites. Jesus was executed by those who regarded him as being in similar **disgrace**. In this way the authorities tried to keep the unclean or disgraced persons away from the people as a whole. To this day there are leaders in the Jewish community who are intent on keeping the story of Jesus from their people, preferring to keep him 'outside of the camp'.

Before we follow up this last point it is important to mention

one further layer of significance in the image of sacrifice
outside of the camp. Earlier in this letter (9:11-14) *Hebrews*
referred to the sacrifice of the Red Heifer for purification.
The body of this sacrificed animal was also to be burned
outside the camp. Perhaps we have an allusion here to Jesus
as the supreme sacrifice for purification in our lives?

To return to the matter of the disgrace of being executed
outside of the camp, or city gate in this case, it is vital to
notice the conviction of *Hebrews* that those who follow Jesus
must also **go to him outside the camp.** We must be there
with Jesus **bearing the disgrace he bore** if we are to really
belong to him. Jesus himself said:

> anyone who does not carry his cross and follow me cannot be my
> disciple (Luke 14:27).

Jesus died as a man rejected by many of his own people, leaders
included, and abused and despised by the brutal Roman
government of the time. His followers will not know the full
joy of commitment to and friendship with him unless they
turn their backs on the security of keeping their faith to
themselves. Paul knew this full well:

> I want to know the Messiah and the power of his resurrection and
> the fellowship of sharing in his sufferings, becoming like him in
> his death, and so, somehow, to attain to the resurrection from the
> dead (Phil. 3:10).

It is entirely possible that some of the Jewish believers who
were receiving this letter were tempted to stay safely 'within
the camp', which is to say that they might have been prepared
to keep quiet about their faith in Jesus as Israel's one and
only Messiah. *Hebrews* is urging them to accept the cost of
discipleship and identify with their Messiah who identified
with them in coming to die for them outside the camp.

The reward of accepting the cost of discipleship is great, however. *Hebrews* reminds his readers in words reminiscent of the previous two chapters that the city which they are called to leave is not an **enduring city**. They are heirs of a glory which others cannot begin to imagine, and so they are **looking for the city that is to come** (see 11:9-10, 13-16; 12:22). The heavenly Jerusalem is more than worth the disgrace they might have for following Jesus.

And so we note that this section of the letter opens and closes with reference to the substantive nature of our faith. Jesus himself is absolutely dependable in the midst of all that life throws at us. He is **the same yesterday and today and for ever**. The home which we will share with him is, in contrast with the earthly Jerusalem or any other place, **an enduring city**. Our lives are safe in the Lord's hands, and we can trust him to take care of us if we rely on his grace.

41. The sacrifices of faith (13:15-16)

In a very creative manner *Hebrews* follows this last section on the once and for all self-sacrifice that Jesus made, a sacrifice which makes all other sacrificial and ceremonial offerings 'of no value', with a section where he focuses on what believers can and should offer to the Lord. These **sacrifices**, using the word in a metaphorical sense, are to be made **continually**, because **God is pleased** with them. Paul makes the same point in Romans 12:1 where he speaks about our bodies being offered to God as our 'spiritual worship'.

The sacrifices stated here have nothing to do with the search for redemption or forgiveness, but are rather offered out of gratitude to God for what he has done in our lives and in the context of our desire to please him and to try to live our lives in imitation of Jesus. Four distinct ways in which we can offer God our lives are given in these verses.

First of all, and of fundamental importance, is the **sacrifice of praise**. In the days of the tabernacle and the temple there were thanksgiving offerings, specified in Leviticus 7:12-15. We see an instance of them being offered in Psalm 116:17 (see also Ps. 50:12-14, 23). God does not need anything from us, but the sin of ingratitude to God is a most serious one. There never will come a time when it will not be appropriate to praise the Lord for his sovereign rule in our lives.

Indeed there is a famous Jewish midrash on the Levitical passages which makes this very point, and *Hebrews'* readers would have been familiar with this teaching:

> Rabbi Pinchas, Rabbi Levi and Rabbi Yochanan said in the name of Rabbi Menachem of Gallia: 'In the Age to come all sacrifices will be annulled except for the sacrifice of thanksgiving' (Leviticus Rabbah 9:7).

God is enthroned on the praises of his people, as it says in Scripture, and God is worthy to be praised. This conviction has even influenced Jewish and Christian attitudes towards times of worship, in that services are designed to open with praise of God before moving on to any other dimension of worship. The basic prayer in the synagogue service, known as the Amidah, a prayer of petition and intercession as well as thanksgiving, is prefaced by the words of Psalm 51:15:

> O Lord, open my lips, and my mouth will declare your praise.

In many Protestant church traditions these same words are used as a preface to the preaching of the sermon. The point is that all our worship of God, all our prayer and communication with him should be couched in praise as the only appropriate way to address him. Other people don't give thanks to the Father of Jesus (Rom. 1:21), and so it is our responsibility, as well as our joy, to make sure that we do.

In some traditions there is a teaching that by 'sacrificing

praise' *Hebrews* must be intending praise that costs us something, since the sacrifice of an animal was always a loss to the person bringing it, either by the loss of an animal from a herd or flock, or because the person had to buy the creature to be sacrificed. By this reasoning, praising God cannot be a sacrifice since it costs nothing – unless there is a type of praise which is costly.

Those who take this line of thinking say that praise can only be a sacrifice when it does not come spontaneously or naturally. In other words, if there are things going on in our lives which are difficult or depressing, etc., then to praise God in such a situation would not be the result of a natural sense of gratitude or trust. It would be a praise which was given by an act of will. It would reflect a profound understanding that God is in control no matter what happens in life, and that he is to be trusted and praised until the time comes, if at all, when we realise why things seemed to go wrong for a while.

This attitude, when held from genuine conviction and devotion, is indeed a profound and inspiring one. It is therefore to be commended. On the other hand, when it is expressed as a result of peer pressure and does not reflect trust, then it can be very damaging to a person's faith and relationship with God. The Scriptures are also full of examples of people who cried out in despair and doubt to God. Such people, in the honesty of their despair and pain, were not condemned by God.

Therefore I would not wish to interpret these verses in *Hebrews* to mean that we must only respond in praise no matter what is going on in either our own lives or the lives of others. On the other hand, to be able to praise in trust, holding on to God in spite of problems, is a gift to be enjoyed and exercised. Those with this gift, if they use it wisely and compassionately, can be a tremendous help to others who maybe give in too readily to moods and setbacks.

Hebrews then speaks about **the fruit of lips that confess his name**. Some believe that this is just a more poetic way of referring to praise. Praise is the 'natural' fruit from mouths which are always talking about the Lord. However, I believe that we are being taken on to a distinct, though related, aspect of speaking out our faith and love. The verb used here and translated as **confess** also gives us the nouns used in the letter at 4:14 and 10:23, and has to do with bearing testimony.

As well as praising God with our lips we are called to bear testimony in word – and in deed – to what he means to us and what he has done for us. We are to glorify his name in the world. For many believers this does appear as a sacrifice, in the sense that they are temperamentally unsuited to speaking to others about their faith. There is a paralysis which seems to come over some believers when they are urged to say something about the Lord to another person. It is one thing to sing and pray in front of other believers, but quite another to speak to a non-believer.

While we should acknowledge and be easy with the fact that not everyone is gifted or called to be 'an evangelist' in any special sense, it is also the case that believers are to be expected to be able to give a simple word of personal testimony when the situation arrives. It will cost some believers more than it does others, but it is a way to honour the Lord which is available in one way or another to all believers.

It may be that some of the recipients of this letter were counting that very cost and were tempted to keep quiet about their faith so as not to get in trouble. This may have been a contributory factor in the temptation of some of them to stop meeting for worship and fellowship (10:25). It is always easier to keep one's faith to oneself. Yet Jesus himself warned about the reverse cost, as it were. Speaking of a situation where there could be serious repercussions for acknowledging one's commitment to him, Jesus said:

Whoever acknowledges me before men, I will also acknowledge
him before my Father in heaven. But whoever disowns me before
men, I will disown him before my Father in heaven (Matt. 10:32-
33).

Next, *Hebrews* says, **do not forget to do good**. These words
come after a number of verses speaking about sacrifices and
ceremonial foods, but it would have come as no surprise to
these Jewish believers. *Hebrews* is simply standing in the well
established line of biblical and Jewish thinking which has
always seen the love of God and love for one another as
inseparable in God's eyes. People like to separate the two,
but as John writes:

If anyone says, 'I love God', yet hates his brother, he is a liar. For
anyone who does not love his brother, whom he has seen, cannot
love God, whom he has not seen. And he has given us this
command: Whoever loves God must also love his brother (1 John
4:20-21).

John is restating a basic prophetic teaching which is known
to all Jewish people as well as Christians. Two famous
expressions of this teaching in the prophetic books are the
following:

For I desire mercy, not sacrifice, and acknowledgment of God
rather than burnt offerings (Hos. 6:6).

He has showed you, O man, what is good. And what does the
LORD require of you? To act justly and to love mercy and to walk
humbly with your God (Mic. 6:8).

The prophets were not hostile to the temple and the sacrificial
system, as some Christians have tried to teach, because the
temple, the priesthood and the system of sacrifices was God's
good purpose from the beginning. What they railed against
was the way in which some people would abuse the system to
the extent that they believed that they could live their lives

just as they wanted, treat other people badly, but be all right
with God because they came to the temple and offered the
right sacrifices.

The truth is that God demands both love for himself and
for other people. Jesus also underlined this for us when he
was asked what the greatest commandment in Scripture was.
He replied by quoting from two passages in the Hebrew Bible,
linking two commandments inseparably:

> 'Teacher, which is the greatest commandment in the Law?' Jesus
> replied: 'Love the Lord your God with all your heart and with all
> your soul and with all your mind. This is the first and greatest
> commandment. And the second is like it: Love your neighbour as
> yourself. All the Law and the Prophets hang on these two
> commandments' (Matt. 22:36-40).

Putting love for others into action might be called 'doing
good', and although we shy from that expression these days
because of its overtones of trying to earn salvation by good
works or of interfering in people's lives, it was a fine
expression for *Hebrews* to use. Jesus told his followers:

> let your light shine before men, that they may see your good deeds
> and praise your Father in heaven (Matt. 5:16).

Paul instructed the congregations which he taught to make
sure that they were keeping this command of Jesus':

> Therefore, as we have opportunity, let us do good to all people,
> especially to those who belong to the family of believers (Gal.
> 6:10. See also Eph. 2:10).

Hebrews and his congregation would also have imbibed this
godly perspective from their Jewish roots. One of the most
famous teachings in the ethical tractate, 'The Sayings of the
Fathers', reflects this biblical emphasis:

Simon the Just was one of the last survivors of the Great Assembly. He used to say, 'The world is based on three things: the Torah, the worship of God and deeds of loving kindness' (1:2).

After the destruction of the temple in 70 AD the Jewish people were unable to offer sacrifices, and so the leaders of the Jewish community developed what might be called a theology of dispensation in the interim period until the rebuilding of the temple. They decided that in lieu of the sacrifices God would accept a combination of three things: genuine repentance for sin, prayer for Israel and the world, and acts of loving kindness.

Note how in all of the above examples the care for one another was not allowed to be separated from the worship of God. This is a spiritual lesson still to be deeply learned by all believers. In what way might this be seen as a sacrifice? Jesus himself taught us to be sacrificial in our desire to bless others and help them – even if they are not well disposed towards us:

If someone wants to sue you and take your tunic, let him have your cloak as well. If anyone forces you to go one mile, go with him two miles (Matt. 5:40-41).

Finally, in this section, *Hebrews* says **do not forget... to share with others**. This might simply be, on one level, a reinforcement of what he has just said about 'doing good'. However there is likely to be more to it than that. The word translated here by 'sharing' is from a root which has become well known in English transliteration of the Greek. It is the word *koinonia*. This is usually translated by or understood as 'fellowship' when used by Christian groups.

But this very root gave the term in the early church for financial offerings on behalf of others in need. *Hebrews* might well have this in mind here, thinking of the need to support other believers in worse circumstances than their own. They must resist the temptation to hold on to *everything* which they have in case they might need it one day. They are to share what they have. This can be a sacrifice for some believers.

Paul spoke more openly about this expression of care within the community of believers when he wrote to the Corinthians:

Now about the collection for God's people: Do what I told the Galatian churches to do. On the first day of every week, each one of you should set aside a sum of money in keeping with his income, saving it up, so that when I come no collections will have to be made (1 Cor. 16:1-2).

Each man should give what he has decided in his heart to give, not reluctantly or under compulsion, for God loves a cheerful giver (2 Cor. 9:7).

Giving our tithes and offerings to our local congregations and to societies dedicated to mission, etc., is an important part of our life as believers. We should not simply give our money and forget about it, but should rather give it prayerfully and gladly, trusting that it will be used to help other believers and to bring the gospel to others.

42. Two prayer requests (13:18-19, 23)

Hebrews aligns himself with the other leaders of this congregation (verse 17) and on behalf of all of them he makes a simple and humble request of his people – **pray for us**. Like all leaders he needs to rely not only on grace from the Lord, given directly, as it were, but also on the prayerful support of others.

This prayer request is made in the context of his **desire to live honourably in every way**. The pressures of leadership are serious, and sometimes intense and difficult to bear. *Hebrews* says that they have **a clear conscience**, and his prayer is that they be upheld in their righteous lives. This will relate both to their own personal lives and walk with the Lord and also to the way in which they exercise leadership over the congregation.

Hebrews then goes on to make a more personal request for prayer. This means a very great deal to him, as we see from his words, **I particularly urge you to pray**. The word which lies behind the translation '*particularly* urge' is the same one which *Hebrews* used in the letter at 2:1, where he urged them to 'pay *more careful* attention' to the word of God. This is a strong expression, and underlines the vital importance of studying the word of God and praying for one another.

And what is it that matters so much to *Hebrews*? He asks for prayer that he **may be restored to you soon**. The pastor dearly wishes to be back with his congregation, the more so because of the difficult situation in which they were living. But why should that need prayer? Some have believed that he himself might be in prison or under some form of house arrest. Interestingly, Paul shared a similar hope at one point: 'Prepare a guest room for me, because I hope to be restored to you in answer to your prayers' (Philemon 22).

In spite of this, Paul was not released from his life of house arrest and prison until his execution. Against this interpretation of *Hebrews*' need for prayer, however, are his words in verse 23 where he lets us know that **our brother Timothy** had certainly been imprisoned, but that he has now been **released**. Then *Hebrews* says that it is possible that he might come to visit them with Timothy if Timothy **arrives soon** to where he is.

Whatever the reason for the difficulty of getting to his people, and it may simply be that he was waiting for Timothy at the place where he was being held, we do not know whether or not *Hebrews* was restored to his people. *Hebrews* cannot have been sure either at the time of writing the letter whether he would see them soon. And so we see the context for his prayer for them which follows.

43. A closing blessing (13:20-21)

Whatever the circumstances of their lives from this point on, the community is never to forget that their God is a **God of peace**. This concept, which we have already explored elsewhere, means that God will be seeking to bring order and wholeness into their lives. Even if it is chaotic all around them, their inner beings can rest in the knowledge that God is in control of their lives and that he will lead them in the best paths for them.

This concept probably also indicates that God will help the believers to act with integrity in their relationships in the world even if the world is less than honest and honourable towards them (see 12:14).

But *Hebrews* is also praying here that God will do something quite specific for the community of believers. He prays that he will **equip** them in order to do God's will. We cannot really be expected to do God's will if we are simply left to our own resources, and so we need to ask for the gift of God's grace to enable us. The word used in the Greek actually means 'to put something into proper order or condition', and *Hebrews* may be asking the Lord to do just that for his people.

He is asking God to give them the gifts and grace necessary to get their lives in order so that they can serve him completely. This is a big prayer, and one which we should not be afraid of making for ourselves and others. *Hebrews* prays that God will give them whatever it takes to be able to serve him – **everything good for doing his will**.

This, at any rate, is the common understanding of this section of the prayer. But an alternative understanding may in fact be more fitting here. *Hebrews* has opened this prayer in an appeal to the **God of peace**, and I believe that we should be expecting more of a matching thought in the second part of the prayer. There is an old Jewish spiritual and moral conviction that one of the fundamental ways in which we can try to comprehend what God is doing in our world is to think of it as 'tikkun olam'. This means, 'repairing the world'.

God is at work in the world restoring it to fellowship with himself, restoring the true worship of God in the world, repairing all the hurts and broken relationships, etc. It is a beautiful and profound theological perspective, and may have been very well known to the Jewish believers then, whether by that name or not. This would make a lovely complement to the first part of the prayer with its emphasis on peace and wholeness.

Significantly, the Greek verb translated by 'equip' can also be used in the sense of 'restoring' or 'repairing'. It is used famously in Matthew 4:21 for the repairing of the fishermen's nets after they were torn. *Hebrews* may have been praying that God would restore their broken confidence, or their damaged faith, or their strained relationships in the face of the pressures around them. A community which has itself experienced the healing and restoration of the Lord can reach out to the wider world with the Good News of God's love and power.

Repairing the world begins with repairs in the family of God. With such a community of believers God can **work in us what is pleasing to him**. However, even here the gifting of God becomes available to us only **through the blood of the eternal covenant**, expounded to the believers in the heart of the letter. The resurrection of Jesus **from the dead** is the key matter here, as *Hebrews* understood well.

Jesus is given one of his most wonderful titles in this prayer – the **great Shepherd of the sheep**. *Hebrews* is reminding his readers that the God who would restore them and prepare them for service in the hostile world around them was the loving Father of Jesus. The Son of their God would be the caring Shepherd whom they would need to care for them as they sought to serve God in the world.

For this title and understanding of Jesus we are drawn to John 10:1-18. This passage picks up on some famous passages in the Hebrew Bible, of course, such as Psalm 23 and Isaiah 53:6. Peter also realises the importance of knowing Jesus as our Shepherd in times of trouble and confusion (1 Pet. 2:25). He makes all things possible.

Closing words (13:22, 24-25)

At the end of the letter we are reminded of the pastoral heart of *Hebrews* towards his friends, his brothers and sisters in the Lord Jesus. He could have written much more, opening up his heart to them, but he has disciplined himself to write **only a short letter**. But in it he has concentrated his encouragements, his **word of exhortation**. And he has set out to **urge** them to listen carefully to his words.

The believers are also encouraged to be encouragers themselves – a true leader is always urging his/her people to go beyond themselves to think of others. So they are to **greet** their **leaders** and **all God's people**.

And the final words are as fitting a way for any of us to end our letters to one another as you could find. Indeed they make a wonderful way to end this very commentary: **grace be with you all!**